WORKING WITH
MUSEUMS

WORKING WITH
MUSEUMS

Edited by Timothy Ambrose

**SCOTTISH
MUSEUMS
COUNCIL**

Her Majesty's Stationery Office
Edinburgh

The Scottish Museums Council is an independent company, principally funded by the Secretary of State for Scotland. The Council's purpose is to improve the quality of local museum and gallery provision in Scotland. This it endeavours to do by providing a wide range of advice, services and financial assistance to its membership in the independent and local authority sectors.

Scottish Museums Council
County House
20-22 Torphichen Street
Edinburgh
EH3 8JB

Preface

No museum is an island, and in a fast-changing leisure and educational environment, no museum can afford to be isolationist in its work. More and more, museums are dependent on working with other organisations or each other to effect improvements in the quality and range of services which they provide their users, and in the quality of care with which they look after their collections. One of the most encouraging trends in the Scottish and UK Museums Service in recent years has been the growing awareness of the benefits of the collaborative approach to meet objectives and to effect progress. Such an approach will continue to grow in importance as museums become increasingly involved in economic and community development in the future. At the same time working with others helps to develop new priorities and new ideas which can lead to beneficial change and improvements in the museum service itself.

This volume presents five papers which focus attention on museums working with other institutions and organisations in the following fields – tourism, industry, contemporary arts, universities and education. The contributors discuss different forms of collaboration which bring mutual benefits and illustrate their papers with models of good working practice drawn from many sources. Another five papers explore how museums work with each other in a partnership approach at national, regional and local level to improve professional standards in cost-efficient and cost-effective ways.

All of these papers are written by contributors who are well known specialists in their fields. They were given at a Scottish Museums Council conference held in Edinburgh at the Royal Museum of Scotland in November 1987. Together they provide a description of current practice in museums and prescriptions for the future. That future will depend for its success on effective collaboration between museums and their partners-in-action.

Timothy Ambrose
Acting Director
Scottish Museums Council
February 1988

Contents

Introduction

Trevor Clark

Trevor Clark was Chairman of the Scottish
Museums Council for 1981–1984, and was elected
again to this position in 1987. He is also an
Edinburgh City Councillor, and a former Trustee
of the National Museums of Scotland and
Museums Association Councillor.

This publication is really about **Partnership**. That is symbolised by the local and independent museums' representative body, the Scottish Museums Council, having held their conference on which this publication is based in the National Museums' stately flagship, the Royal Museum of Scotland. I have been advised that a more suitable Buzzword of the Age for Great Experts to employ, rather than Partnership, might be **Synergy**. 'Ah, yes', I hear the knowledgeable cry. To one of the dwindling number that was instructed in the linguistic roots of our western Science and Culture, that is a scholarly way of saying **Working Together**; but I have been further advised that Great Experts interpret the word in the sense of the Totality being Greater than the Sum of its Parts – or One Plus One Equals Three, or at least Two point Something. An outdated educational system recognised that too – it simply means the Team Spirit, Chaps. What gets Pittodrie to lick Tynecastle, or vice versa (I'll translate for our foreign friends, what enables Somerset to skittle out Yorkshire, though not very often). I looked synergy up in a dictionary, incidentally, and found that one Melanchthon, a liberal Protestant reformer who once advised Henry VIII to take two wives, may have propounded the doctrine of **Synergism**, suggesting that the human will and the divine spirit are two efficient agents that co-operate in regeneration. So Synergism let it be, and I'll tell you why.

We have ten distinguished human spirits listed here. Five are friends from five worlds closely linked to our own. They offer us valuable thoughts on how we can scratch each others' backs and make each successive pair of those worlds better places, both for us inside them and for the punters outside who pay for us. And five are toilers in our own vineyards (taking time off from protecting Chardonnay and Cabernet-Sauvignon from phylloxera). They show us how to take in each others' washing and end up with a really splendid display on the clothesline – the economics of that being that some folk are better at boiling and starching dress shirts, and others more suited to popping non-iron polyester undies into the tumble-dryer. But even ten human spirits don't make a full team, we need eleven players; and synergism did presuppose in addition a divine will. I'm only the referee; I can't complete the squad of partners. What is missing is the voice of management from heaven, the master of our fates, the captain of our souls, the Divine Will.

In 1872 there was established a formal committee of Her Majesty's Privy Council, to be called the Scotch

Education Department (it only became Scottish in 1918, which is too recent for us in the heritage industry to tak tent of). Like its counterpart down south, the Office of Arts and Libraries, the Scotch civil service actually has a policy for the arts. I think I can paraphrase it pretty directly for reading from my pulpit, though I haven't had time to make it a metrical psalm:

> I shall nourish the love of the learning of my own land, and the works of her men of art.
> In times of trial I shall open the gates of beauty and joy to the wretched of spirit.
> The stranger and the unbeliever, the toiler and the caster of bread upon water, all shall be bidden to our shores.
> Thus shall I feed our young lambs, that are hungering for lush pastures;
> And so shall our people again find that bread, and their talents be returned, manifold.
> But let me not as a wetnurse clasp the child close to my own breast;
> Rather free those that have wisdom and who rejoice in the truth, to share the nurture among our sons and daughters.
> And let the craftsmen and the scribes in our cities, and the herdsmen and reapers in the desert places, witness and love the others' works:
> That glory shall prevail in the gardens.
> Let the multitude and the lonely alike find full favour in my sight;
> And let none falter in adding to the store of knowledge of our forefathers, nor in telling abroad the good news thereof.

If you want to have that in Sir Humphrey (Appleby's) own words, I've got them. Come and see me in my study after school. I hope he realises that that is what he says he wants. But although we don't have Sir Humphrey or one of his Bernards on the list to reassure us, I am in no doubt that the Scotch Education Department understands that we all want to work with them too, as partners, in an act of synergism (or just synergy even). We have to work together, in two-way mutual trust, as efficient agents to co-operate in regeneration of Scotland's and the museums movement's souls. I'm sure the OAL down south knows it too. I am confident that the government's obedient servants and we can achieve this as friends.

Part 1
Museums working with other Institutions and Organisations

Crathes Castle, Kincardine & Deeside.

National Trust for Scotland.

Museums and Tourism

Lester Borley

Lester Borley was Chief Executive of the Scottish Tourist Board from 1970 and Chief Executive of the English Tourist Board from 1975. He is currently the Director of the National Trust for Scotland.

In my paper on 'Museums and Tourism' I dwell partly on the nature of tourism and the nature of museums, going on to consider the nature of communication and the nature of co-operation. Nowhere else on the agenda for the conference was I able to find the words 'Leisure' and 'Recreation', and in my paper I believe it would be sensible to combine them with tourism, in respect of the needs of people.

Professor Brian Morris, at the launch of the Museums and Galleries Commission's Annual Report for 1986/87 said:

'There is a danger that museums and galleries will be seen simply as part of the entertainment industry, providing tourists with somewhere to go when it rains.'

I am sure that entertainment as such is not an inappropriate activity for museums.

The tourist is much maligned. He was caricatured once in a cartoon in the "New Yorker" which showed two Americans leaping from their car, running up the steps of the Louvre and saying to the startled guard:

'Quick, which way to the Mona Lisa. We're doubled parked!'

If we go back even further to the writings of the American Thomas Starr King in 1860, who commented acidly that summer travellers:

'Bolted the scenery, as a man driven by work bolts his dinner . . . sometimes they will gobble some of the superb views between trains, with as little consciousness of any flavour of artistic relish, as a turkey has in swallowing corn.'

So much for the downside. But let us consider what Lord Curzon had to say in India:

'Tourism is a University in which the Scholar never takes his Degree. It is a temple where the suppliant adores but never catches sight of the object of his devotion. It is a journey the goal of which is always in sight, but never attained. There are always learners, always worshippers, always pilgrims.'

In preparing my notes for this paper I never imagined that I would find relevant material in the Financial

Times. Another view on the role of museums was attributed to Anthony D'Offay, a gallery owner who said:

'I believe the idea of contemporary art fulfills some spiritual function in people's lives. In the past we built great cathedrals. Now we build great museums. People worship in galleries as they used to worship in churches.'

So there we have a diversity of opinion and definition regarding both the purposes of museums and the nature of tourism. Museums and tourism have both been subjects of spontaneous combustion in the past twenty years.

However we need to remember that tourism is not the only source of visitors to museums. In its 'Museums are for People' report, the Area Museums Service for South East England stressed that:

'Whilst much has been made of attracting tourists, the backbone of use is local.'

Tourism can often justify a degree of additional development or a special seasonal exhibition, but the majority of use will be by people living within a very limited radius.

The explosion of museums is incredible. Half of the 2,000 museums in the United Kingdom have been created since 1971, attracting over 68 million visitors a year. Overseas visitors represent 24% of that total, indicating the relevance and importance of museums to the business of tourism.

However there is very keen competition for the time of visitors. Museums are in competition with historic buildings, gardens, wildlife and natural resources, and a very large miscellaneous category of tourist attractions. If we take them all together, there was in the last year a total of over 200 million visits paid to such attractions, which suggests a very important public need to be fulfilled.

At the same time there has been a great explosion of tourism, together with increased leisure and recreation opportunities. Tourism has a total turnover in the United Kingdom of about £13 billion per annum. Figures quoted at the opening of the recent InterBuild Exhibition showed that £2 billion were invested in tourism capital projects last year, and £400 million had been spent in the first quarter of 1987 on tourism related projects.

One can only ask 'are you getting your share?' and perhaps 'are you also spending your share'. There is no doubt that to continue to appeal to the general public, whether resident or visitors from further afield, one must move with the times.

All museums are of course paid for by the public in some way. National museums are paid by taxes, local museums by rates or rate support grants, and private and independent museums by admissions or charitable support. This is very much the case for example with the properties owned and maintained by the National Trust for Scotland, which also fulfil a vital tourism function.

Local Government does not often realise that museums can make a positive contribution to the local economy and are as worthy of promotion as any industrial estate.

Tourism expenditures include something like £6,705 million from 13.7 million overseas visitors, and £7,150 million from domestic visitors, 39 million of whom were recorded as being on holidays of 4+ days, and 32 million on short breaks of 1-3 days. If you take this together with the fact that 24.5 million British go abroad, and are exposed to the standards of excellence and attractions in other countries, then you will realise that this is a most important market to be attracted and satisfied.

What about the nature of tourism. Are the needs of a tourist so different from those of a local resident? A tourist is really no more than a displaced person. You may remember George Bernard Shaw once saying that he:

'disliked feeling at home when he was abroad'.

One is transported by aircraft thousands of miles to a destination, and it would be true to say that the majority of visitors have no real idea of where they are in the world. Relatively few people have the knowledge to appreciate to the full what they see, and the majority are satisfied at a very superficial level, especially if there is a language barrier to be overcome. There is therefore a very real need for those responsible for museums and other tourist attractions to realise that they can act effectively as orientation centres, perhaps leading the visitor on to other destinations, which will amplify or fulfil an interest stimulated originally within the museum.

There is of course a popular misconception that all tourists travel in groups. I suppose we have to thank Thomas Cook for that. In fact I think we should really lay the blame at the door of Geoffrey Chaucer. His Canterbury Pilgrims undertook a most amusing if protracted journey to Canterbury and were just a handful among millions who made that pilgrimage over the centuries. In 1420, which was the 250th anniversary of the martyrdom of St. Thomas à Beckett, Canterbury was invaded by 100,000 tourists, which caused the populace to complain. Possibly the only residents who were complacent were the monks who provided the overnight accommodation.

It is interesting that now Canterbury is contemplating the establishment of a museum about Canterbury Pilgrims, so the story of tourism has itself become the attraction.

The National Trust for Scotland's research shows that only 4% of our visitors arrived in organised groups, which compares perhaps with the 10% average recorded by the Scottish Tourist Board. However 67% of our visitors formed part of a small party or a family visit.

Incidentally 68% of our visitors were on holiday and 30% were making a visit as part of a day out from home. Regardless of the nature of the visitor they shared the same characteristic that they had only travelled about 35 miles from their home or overnight accommodation. 89% of them travel by car, which shows that one has to be aware of the need for ancillary facilities for visitors.

It was the Duke of Bedford who said that if he provided an ample car park, an attractive restaurant, very clean toilets and an appealing shop, then 83% of the visitors to Woburn would be blissfully unaware that he also had a stately home. The problem of facilitation of the ancillary needs of visitors is nevertheless most important if people are going to gain full satisfaction from the primary reason for the visit to the museum or attraction.

One cannot stress too much the importance of market research. In the Museums Data Base published recently by the Museums Association 13% of the museums do not actually record admissions, and 6% merely estimate their totals. I was also surprised to learn that 58% of national museums have never done a visitor survey, and that was true also of 67% of local museums and 69% of the other categories of museum.

If the current use or expectation of the visitor is not known or researched how can Museum Directors be sure they are offering the right facilities or attractions? 70% of museums apparently produce free leaflets, up to

Clann'ic Lachlainn Clann'ill Eathain
Clann'ic Leoid Ratharsair
Clan MacLachlan, MacLean
and Raasay MacLeod

Site interpretation for visitors at the battlefield of Culloden.

National Trust for Scotland.

14

20% of those in foreign languages. But how can one be sure what to produce or what to say if there is no research to guide the process.

One needs to promote or publicise a museum from a base of sound knowledge. Research is far less costly than any other essential service, but of considerable importance.

In the work in the National Trust for Scotland we place great emphasis on the need for good market research. For example in the United Kingdom as a whole only 17% of the population may be defined as AB. The NTS membership survey shows that no less than 84% of its members are AB, whilst the research at our properties shows that 44% of our visitors are AB. Therefore we can show that our properties are reaching a wider community. It would be false to assume because our members were of a certain type, that we were catering exclusively for them. This is a most important point of policy when one comes to consider the nature of funding and support which we get from others in the community, who share our objectives of reaching a broad cross section of people.

How then should one consider relating a museum to the formal structure of tourism. To begin with there is the network of Area Tourist Boards and Tourist Offices of District Councils, which feed into the network offered by the Scottish Tourist Board in this country and the British Tourist Authority overseas. In addition we find it important to work in collaboration with transportation companies, car rental firms, hotel groups and also other tourist attractions.

The free exchange of information between ourselves and other houses and historic properties open to the public is maintained through the mechanism of the Scottish Heritage Liaison Group which freely exchanges data about visitor numbers and plans for future promotion. This recognises that the ordinary member of the public does not distinguish between the ownership of properites. To serve his interests and to derive maximum benefit in return there is no point in adopting a competitive position with other owners of tourist attractions. There is only good to be gained from collaboration.

What then is the expectation of the tourist? I have said earlier that he needs orientation, but he also needs the skills of interpretation, and in this sense I do not mean language interpretation necessarily.

Again the Area Museums Service of the South East of England in its report said:

> 'the (Museum) profession is too introspective, and members should be encouraged to travel and broaden their knowledge of visitor requirements'.

A museum has been defined as 'a building dedicated to the pursuit of learning or the arts'. The same dictionary reference goes on to say that a 'museum piece' is 'something worthy of exhibition in a museum'. Also, in a derogatory sense, it is an antiquated or outdated specimen.

What do we mean when we use the word Interpretation. Freeman Tilden, the guru of the U.S. National Park Service, made it clear in an admirable book on the subject that 'the chief aim of Interpretation is not Instruction but Provocation'. It is above all important to provoke and not to bore. I submit that the concept of entertainment is an important one for museums.

It is also important to be careful in the use of language. Walter Savage Landor in his book 'Imaginary Conversations' said:

> 'I have been careful to retain as much idiom as I could. Often at the peril of being called ordinary and vulgar. Nations in a state of decay lose their idiom.

Speaking to the people, I use the people's phraseology'.

I think that probably is something we should all follow.

Perhaps it would be helpful to bear in mind that the Ten Commandments are expressed in only 279 words, and the American Declaration of Independence is simply expressed in only 300 words.

Henry Ford once declared that 'History is bunk'. However tourism research indicates that an interest in history and countryside are the principal motivators of international Travel. The growth and nature of museums open between 1976 and 1985 would seem to bear this out. Dr. David Prince has pointed out that a new museum opens every fortnight, and most are privately run or independent-charity funded museums of social history, rural society history, technology and transport or industrial archaeology.

This certainly echoes the National Trust for Scotland policy, as we are taking an increasing interest in the social history of the 19th and 20th centuries. This is most manifest in our properties such as the Angus Folk Museum, the Pitmedden Museum of Rural Life, the farm courtyard complex at the House of Dun, Robert Smail's Printing Works at Innerleithen, and the new display in preparation at Leith Hall on the theme 'For Crown and Country', which will illustrate the military careers of that landed family.

Our education programme is geared to communicating the social story of properties such as Gladstone's Land, Culzean Castle, and our plans for Falkland and Culross will certainly be reaching out to people's understanding of the history of these communities. Out new exhibition 'The Kingdom of the Scots' at Bannockburn tries to illustrate the 300 years of the flowering of the Scottish culture following the Wars of Independence.

There is need for a constant exchange and dialogue between museums and other attractions. The National Trust for Scotland has benefited from a magnificent exhibition in the Royal Museum of Scotland entitled 'Treasures in Trust'. We have lent our silver from Brodick to Aberdeen, the Treasures of Fyvie were displayed at the Scottish National Portrait Gallery in Edinburgh and subsequently at Agnews in London. We have lent pictures to the Watteau exhibition in Paris, the Winterhalter exhibition at the National Portrait Gallery, and Mrs. Gregory by Raeburn adorned the underground poster hoardings when her picture appeared at the Tate Gallery.

We have given help to the National Museums of Scotland in the development of their shops policy, whilst they have given us much support with our conservation work.

There is scope for the exchange of materials and ideas at all levels.

May I now turn to the standards of excellence which tourists who travel world-wide might consider to be the touchstones for the future. I would suggest the Smithsonian Institution in Washington D.C. not only for its Air and Space Museum, which attracts over 10 million visitors a year, but more importantly its Museum of American History, and its newly opened Museum of African Art, as part of the Arthur Sackler complex. The Art in Industry Museum in Washington, a pastiche of the 1873 exhibition in Philadelphia is well worth study.

In Europe I have found the Heimatmuseums in Bavaria, particularly in Munich and Nuremberg to be outstanding. Those who have stood in the Viking Museum at Roskilde looking out over the water where the original Viking ships were found or wondered at the tessellated pavements in the Baldo Museum in Tunis know that the best ideas are the simple ones.

If one is looking for examples of what is called the living museum then I think Old Sturbridge in Massachusetts, which takes the years 1780 – 1820 as its period is worth attention. Certainly the American Museum at Bath always gives me an American experience quite distinct from that which one finds in neighbouring Bath museums.

In terms of special exhibitions one recalls the outstanding Bedouin exhibition put on by the Museum of Mankind in London some years age. The greatest compliment I can pay to it is that when I subsequently went into the Souks of Sfax, Fez and Samarkand I was reminded of the smells and atmosphere created in the Museum of Mankind in London.

In conclusion could I say that the importance and relevance of tourism to museums must be understood. There is a need for knowledge, and a need for provocation if one is to take full advantage of these economic benefits of tourism. There is also the need to relate to others and the synergy which is possible between unlikely partners should be explored.

Above all we should echo the words of William Blake when we hope that the visitor might:

> 'See a World in A Grain of Sand
> And a Heaven in a Wild Flower
> Hold Infinity in the Palm of His Hand
> And Eternity in an Hour'.

But may I add a cautionary tailpiece from Anatole France who said:

> 'Do not try to satisfy your vanity by teaching a great many things. Awaken people's curiosity. It is enough to open minds; do not overload them. Put there just a spark. If there is some good inflammable stuff, it will catch fire'.

'The most successful industrial achievement in Britain today.' Shell Esso Brent Charlie Production Platform.   *Shell UK Exploration and Production.*

Museums and Industry

John Moorhouse

John Moorhouse is the Head of Public Affairs of Shell UK Exploration and Production. He has been with the Shell Group since 1963. He is Chairman of Community Task Force and Young Enterprise (Grampian), Deputy Chairman of the Aberdeen Enterprise Trust and a member of the Executive Committee of Scottish Business in the Community.

Throughout the world museums have chronicled the history of Industry, sped in recent years by the frenetic growth of the so-called 'Heritage Industry'. I believe that in this country a new museum or heritage centre has opened every ten days for the past decade.

As Chairman of Community Task Force, one of the largest Managing Agencies under the Manpower Services Commission's Community Programme, I know that these developments have excellent opportunities for giving training and work in an enormously wide range of disciplines for many thousands of men and women. CTF itself has been involved in dozens of heritage-linked schemes, ranging from a one-room interpretative centre in the Pennine village of Housesteads to the complete restoration and re-building of the splendid Victorian cast iron and timber pier which projects one-third of a mile into the Menai Strait from Bangor in North Wales. This last project has employed between 40 and 60 local people for the past five years.

Indeed it was the attractiveness of the gearing provided by the MSC, in creating jobs in an area of high

unemployment, coupled with an imaginative project, which first tempted Shell UK to bend its rules on charitable giving to 'bricks and mortar' appeals. This was when the trustees of the Ironbridge Gorge Museum approached us for help in recreating a wrought-ironworks at the Blists Hill site. The remarkable achievements of a handful of enthusiasts with imagination and clear business acumen led to the success of this appeal.

The recent growth of the Heritage and Museum business though has not been fuelled just by the availability of a construction workforce. It has been to an even greater extent demand led – and the demand will continue to grow. Let me tell you why by using a very personal experience to develop my point.

When I left School, as a young man of seventeen, to join that illustrious organisation F W Woolworth and Co Ltd as a Trainee Manager one cold December morning, I expected to work for them for the rest of my life. Of course, I knew I would become Chairman at least, and retire at the age of 65. A forty-eight year spell. My working week was forty-eight hours, and with two weeks a year holiday and Bank Holidays added, I worked for forty-eight weeks a year. So effectively I had contracted to work for 48 × 48 × 48 = 110,592 hours in my lifetime.

Let us now look at my son, Miles, who at seventeen years of age is still in full time education, expecting to remain there for the next four or even five years. He will (hopefully) start work at twenty-one or twenty-two, retiring at sixty − a total of 38 years. He will probably work a 38-hour week and with six weeks holiday a year, more local and bank holidays and the bonus of self-certificated sick leave, be working nearer 38 weeks a year. So he will contract to work for 38 × 38 × 38 = 54,872 hours.

So, in less than three decades we have seen the working lifetime halved, AND NO-ONE HAS REALLY NOTICED THE DIFFERENCE.

The next two decades could easily see the working lifetime halved again.

We are beginning to see dramatic changes in the balance between working time and leisure time too. Earlier this year for example Shell UK Exploration and Production introduced a revolutionary change to the shift pattern for its Offshore workers. Until this year we operated a seven days on/seven days off cycle, with 'normal' leave and Public Holidays in addition. In February of this year we changed the pattern to one of 14 days on/21 days off, incorporating annual leave and Public Holidays in the resulting ten three-week holidays per annum which these employees enjoy. This example of 'parcelling-up' free time into usable chunks could well be adopted by many other industries operating on a continuous process basis − although the hurdle of getting the necessary twelve-hour working shift accepted may be difficult to surmount.

Certainly the three- or four-day weekend cannot be

very far away. So the greatest challenge and opportunity facing us today is to find appropriate ways of profitably occupying all this extra leisure time. The Museum business, catering as it does so admirably for leisure time, will certainly continue to be demand-led for the forseeable future.

But is it really healthy to concentrate so completely on the past? Is the dreamworld of 'the good old days' the right diet for future generations? Are we very far from the day, proposed by Neil Cossons, when we just charge the tourists an admission fee when they cross the border into Scotland or land at Heathrow − a sort of national Heritage Park called 'Limeyland' or 'UKworld?'

Should we not be creating Museums of the present time and the near future, designed not only to inform but also to inspire the younger generation to be inventive and innovative; to make our present day achievements exciting and relevant to them; to challenge their fertile young minds to conceive greater and better achievements?

For too long, one could argue, British Industry has devoted its limited sponsorship budgets to glorifying the past. Timothy Mason in his paper explains how difficult it is to persuade Industry to support the work of contemporary artists − better to 'invest' in the tried and tested works of the establishment. Similarly in the world of classical music, sponsors virtually queue to back Tchaikovsky, just as the audience will queue to hear his Sixth − but just try to get support for Stockhausen.

Last year was designated Industry Year '86. We all heard, many, many times how Britain has become the worlds only Industrialised Nation with an anti-industry culture. Great efforts were made to redress the balance by forging links with Schools and Industry, but has it been enough?

Could these several points be linked together, I wonder.

The Oil Experience – an impression of the Fun Learning Centre telling the story of North Sea oil and gas.

Shell UK Exploration and Production.

Should industry not be putting its considerable resources of manpower and imagination behind the culture of the future as well as the 'museums of the future' which I noted above?

At present I am proud to be involved in the early stages of the development of such a museum. Subject to all the intervening problems being solved it will tell the story of the most successful industrial achievement in Britain today. A story which has unfolded within the lifetime of us all, and continues to develop in a dramatic and vital way. It is a success on a par with the development of the canals in the eighteenth century, the railways in the nineteenth and the space technology of the USA in the twentieth. It is, of course, the story of North Sea Oil, and the development of this 'Museum of the Future' will be in Aberdeen.

For if Aberdeen is to have a future in the world of tourism, there is a need to change the 'tourist map' of Scotland. At present the route is Edinburgh – Perth – Inverness – turn left – West Coast – Loch Lomond – Glasgow – South. Important work is being done in Dundee – development of Heritage – Discovery – Waterfront etc. Fife's newly signposted 'tourist route' has increased traffic through the Kingdom by about 4% in this its first year.

With these two initiatives having persuaded tourists to turn right at Perth or to enter Tayside by way of the Tay Bridge we need to dissuade tourists from taking the 'Aberdeen By-Pass' (the A9) by creating a huge magnet of an attraction in the North East – which will make a visit to Aberdeen irresistible. The attraction has to be on such a scale that it is spoken of in the same breath as Disneyworld and Epcot. It has to be a 'must' for the majority of visitors to Britain as well as for very many residents of these islands.

This magnet could be 'The Oil Experience'. The *Aberdeen Beyond 2000* Report, recently produced by a group of prominent local businessmen said:

'The Oil Experience would be a themed exposition of the industry from oil and gas formation through to recovery, refining, use and economic impact'.

Initial thoughts are to produce a purpose-built facility designed to take the visitor through the complete offshore experience simulating as closely as possible all the experiences associated with the struggle to extract oil and gas from the North Sea and the human endeavour involved.

Whilst we want this 'experience' to provide a lasting record of the achievements in the North Sea we don't want it to be a museum, in the outmoded sense of the word, or to be a facility only used to remind people of these achievements. We want it to be an entertaining place that people travel far to visit. We have based our philosophy on 80% entertainment and 20% education, although there is no reason whatsoever why we should not achieve 100% education and 100% fun – perhaps one of our mistakes is believing that the two are mutually exclusive.

We aim to make the maximum use of modern technology to simulate the various experiences – travel in a helicopter, working on a drill floor, descending in a submersible vehicle, possibly even following a drill bit deep into the earth's crust. We need a variety of exhibits, some of which will be pure 'white knuckle' type experiences which the visitor sits through, while others will be where the visitor is able to go 'hands on' and experience the results of his actions.

We are currently developing a conceptual design for the facility, which we see as purpose-built structure, visually exciting in itself and clearly symbolic based on popular and realistic offshore images.

Maybe I should make it clear at this stage that we have reviewed the possibility of the facility being housed in a redundant oil rig moored just off the foreshore and have confirmed that this is not a practicable solution. Mobile drilling rigs of the type we have recently seen moored in Aberdeen Bay bear little relation to the large multi-function fixed platforms from which production wells are drilled and on which the oil and gas is treated for transport to shore. The cost of providing and then maintaining such is very high and access to it would be far from easy. However we did not reject the concept out of hand but re-visited the possibility and convinced ourselves that we should not pursue it.

We see this clearly as a long-term project, one which is going to grow from its initial start and be continually updated with new or modified exhibits to encourage repeat visits. We see it as a National if not International facility rather than simply an Aberdeen or Grampian one, attracting visitors from far afield. We have big ideas and we are committed to converting them into reality.

Such is the attraction envisaged by the Oil Experience Committee of the Aberdeen Beyond 2000 Group. It will make the twentieth century's most exciting and successful commercial adventure come to life in a thrilling, dramatic and educational form. The excitement of a journey offshore. The hostility of the environment 150 miles North-East of Shetland. The magical world of Divers and Submariners. The fantasy of journeying towards the centre of the earth and back through time to discover how oil and gas were created. All this, and more, will be simulated, using the very latest technology, to create a unique, unforgettable experience.

The Oil Experience will hopefully be funded from a range of sources. Clearly there will be room for public sector contributions from one source or another, for the attraction is to be of National and even International importance. The offshore industry itself, both operators and specialist contractors, will have a role too in sponsoring individual 'exhibits' – for example one of the companies involved in diving would be an appropriate supporter for the underwater elements. The third area of finance will be drawn in on a commercial basis – as we expect the Experience to offer excellent value for money to the visitor, as well as a good return for the investor.

The underlying message of my paper is that, in the widest sense, museums have become an industry in themselves, and an industry which has a key role to play not only in the profitable and pleasurable fields of leisure and tourism, but also in the most vital task of influencing and inspiring future generations of industrialists.

IF THE PEOPLE CAN'T GET TO THE GALLERY, WE TAKE THE GALLERY TO THE PEOPLE.

The Travelling Gallery is just one way we go out of our way to make art more accessible to people.

Another is the fact that, thanks to subsidies, most galleries are free.

And much of the real cost of theatre and concert tickets is paid for before you pay for them.

The rest is met by the Scottish Arts Council, local authorities and private sponsors.

Arts subsidies aren't just for artists. They're for everyone.

Scottish Arts Council

Scottish Arts Council/Scottish Provident Travelling Gallery. Visitors watching tape/slide presentation in the gallery.

Antonia Reeve.

The Role of Contemporary Art in Museums

Timothy Mason

Timothy Mason has been Director of the Scottish Arts Council since 1980. Prior to that he was Director of the Western Australian Arts Council. He is a member of the Scottish and Arts Committees of the Britain-Australia Bicentennial Committee.

The way in which the term 'contemporary art' is often sadly used nowadays seems to suggest an art that is markedly different from any art of the past – an art that has no roots, and furthermore, an art that is odd, difficult, unpopular; an art that needs organisations like arts councils to support it because it has insufficient attraction to survive unaided. It is interesting that the only arts which, when prefixed with the adjective 'contemporary', give rise to these doubts, are music and the visual arts. Contemporary literature, contemporary drama, even contemporary dance, are neutral, perhaps even positive, terms – they are merely the work that is being done now rather than that of a past time.

Perhaps that is because music and the visual arts are the two art forms whose creations in this century have been most concerned with formal qualities and where 'modernism' has been most influential. Modernism is of course now much discredited. We are now all post-modernists or even post post-modernists. But modernism was based on the premise that art developed, not just in its social and economic

relationship with society but formally, within itself. This led artists to experiment with the form of work rather than the content, or rather the form became the content. Since Cezanne, artists could respectably concern themselves with the picture frame and the paint surface rather than with representation. This inevitably led to the minimalist and conceptional art of the late sixties and early seventies. This was probably what gave 'contemporary art' its worst connotations. In the public eye, and perhaps more important in the eye of the popular press, modern art was weird enough (women with three eyes and noses on the sides of their heads) but this contemporary art was clearly the work of charlatans; blank canvases, crushed motor cars, piles of bricks, bad enough to pass these off as art – but then for them to change hands for large sums of money, that was really asking for trouble.

Contemporary art had reached a dead end. It had developed its formal concerns to such an extent that not only did the public lose interest, artists themselves began to lose interest. Worst of all, the market lost interest. Something new was needed and hence post-modernism − it looks back at tradition, it is figurative, it sells. Scotland, particularly Glasgow, is quick to muscle in. We had been a little late to become impressionists, Colquhoun and MacBride, were about 40 years behind their times, our Abstract Expressionists, because of the colour reproductions in Art Form, were only about fifteen years too late and our minimalists and conceptionalists almost, but not quite, made it on time. Now thanks to good local promotion and a sluggish London market, we looked as if we were almost out in front.

But hype or not, contemporary art does look as if it is shedding its stigma. It is attracting audiences, buyers and class again. For proof look in the lobbies of Charlotte Square law firms or the offices of our major industrialists or merchant banks. Among the Peploes and Caddells are now the Bellanys and the Campbells. Respectability again.

The period I have been describing over the last half century has been one where, with some honourable exceptions, museums (and here I am principally talking about local authority museums with art collections) have not involved themselves much with 'contemporary' art. Whatever the reasons have been, this is strange because many of these museums were, when established, right at the forefront of the art that was then contemporary. Take, for the example, the McLean Museum and Art Gallery in Greenock or the McManus Galleries in Dundee or the Kirkcaldy Art Gallery with its collection created by a linoleum baron at the end of the nineteenth century. The great patrons and collectors who endowed so many of our museums and galleries did so with pictures that were then contemporary. In many cases the purchasing policies continued to be contemporary right up to the 1930's and '40's. It is difficult today to make the leap of imagination back to the latter part of the last century and the early part of this, and to see these pictures in their gilt frames as the contemporary art of a previous generation.

But when one makes that leap one cannot but be impressed by the confidence and bravura of that generation. The men responsible were, for the most part, the merchants and industrialists who were serving, and reaping the rewards from, our Empire. They were the same kind of men as the merchants and bankers who made the Florentine renaissance. It was new money buying respectability. They bought old art as well, but they had the confidence to buy new art too. That confidence died with them, bequests dwindled, curators, for some reason, became nervous about the art of their own time. Now local authority committees rather than individuals held the purse strings and contemporary art became something you rarely saw in museums. Some collections are, of course, better than others in this respect but nearly all suffer from this time warp.

But confidence *does* seem to be growing again, the public appears less suspicious of today's art and the majority of curators are trying hard to bring contemporary art back into museums. One strand of thinking which has affected this development − or re-development − has, I believe, been the growing, and much welcome, interest in accessibility and interpretation. As museums have continued to place a greater emphasis on interpreting the objects in their care, so gallery curators have also been encouraged to attempt to explain to their public, developments in contemporary art − and to take greater risks. At the same time, they have revealed, or developed, a personal commitment to the art in their care and have recognised the need to bridge the gap between some contemporary art and its potential audience.

This better presentation has had the consequential effect of increasing attendances and has, in some cases, even helped to loosen the purse strings of local authority committees whose members are often beginning to see the benefits this can bring and are enthusiastically supporting their curators in this attempt. These are all developments which the Arts Council has both welcomed and encouraged.

One thinks in particular of Aberdeen, the McLaurin at Ayr, the Smith in Stirling and the City Art Centre in Edinburgh, although there are several others equally progressive. Aberdeen, under the inspired direction of Ian McKenzie Smith, was the first local authority gallery in Scotland to see the possibility of revitalizing itself and offering a visually exciting and welcoming experience for visitors by presenting in its foyer and principal galleries contemporary pictures and sculptures in a way that complements beautifully the building itself and therefore become accepted as part of the place.

At Ayr, Kyle and Carrick District Council has adopted an adventurous policy of assembling a collection of contemporary art at Rozelle House, complemented by a mixed programme of temporary exhibitions in the adjacent galleries. The Smith at Stirling, where both Central Region and Stirling District Council have shown enormous commitment in upgrading the building, has put itself firmly on the cultural map of Scotland through its Biennale which immediately established itself as one of the major open exhibitions for professional artists in Scotland. Edinburgh District Council is now vigorously purchasing the work of Edinburgh artists for its collection housed in the City Art Centre.

The benefits to such galleries and museums are many. The curators and directors of those I have mentioned (and there are more I have not) could, better than I, describe these in detail, but here are some:

First, whether a museum sees its main objective as the accumulation of treasures or the interpretation of cultures, the acquisition and presentation of the art that is being made today must be an essential part of achieving the objective. Not to do so is to deny the museum's public access to a whole area of culture.

Secondly, the atmosphere of a building can be transformed by careful selection and placing of modern pictures and sculpture. The museum's image can be improved enormously in this way. For example, visit Aberdeen Art Gallery on Thursday night – when it's open late. Banners flutter outside the gallery. In the large hall which is the gallery's foyer, there is a fountain; contemporary art fills the space – on one wall, a large Bert Irwin canvas in yellow and orange almost sings on a dreigh November night. The coffee shop is busy, so too is the lively and well-stocked bookshop. It is very much a gallery of today.

Thirdly, a museum's reputation can be boosted. This has huge benefits for the image of the town and the local authority responsible. Visitors from all over the world come to the Pier Arts Centre in the small town of Stromness to see Margaret Gardiner's personal collection of the best of the St. Ives school – including Nicolson, Hepworth and Wallis – housed in a beautiful gallery by the water. It is not simply for artistic or philanthropic reasons that corporations like IBM or Charlotte Square lawyers decorate their reception areas with contemporary art. It is for image enhancement and kudos.

Finally, audiences can be increased and broadened. A programme of changing exhibitions encourages regular visits. Young people are showing great interest in contemporary art and design and by including more of these shows in a gallery's programme more young visitors can be encouraged. Here, Edinburgh's City Art Centre has shown the way, operating almost like a five-screen cinema, presenting a lively series of different exhibitions in its different galleries. Something for everyone.

These benefits can be achieved in a number of ways, by

acquisitions, by temporary exhibitions, by artists in residence in the museum, by lecture series, by workshops and classes, by outreach programmes, by video and by performances, and by good marketing. They are best achieved by a mixture of all of these.

Let's take a brief look at some of these examples, beginning with acquisitions – and by that I mean museums acquiring art of now as well as the art of the past. This, of course, requires a budget and I have already given some examples of how this can be achieved. There is also help available through the Local Museum Purchase Fund and the Contemporary Arts Soceity, which has toiled for many years to bring the art of the day into museums and galleries throughout Britain. The Scottish Arts Council has its own collection of over 2000 contemporary works of art which it is happy to hire to galleries and museums.

Temporary exhibitions are sometimes seen as difficult to achieve. I recognise that many museums and galleries do not have the resources, either financial or human, to make exhibitions themselves but in the area of contemporary art, there are now many subsidised galleries which are creating exhibitions of contemporary art which they would be delighted to tour. Subsidy is available from the Scottish Arts Council towards the already modest hire fees.

The idea of an artist-in-residence in a museum or gallery was pioneered by the National Gallery in London. Since then, the example has been followed at home by Aberdeen, and by the Crawford and Talbot Rice Arts Centres in St. Andrews and Edinburgh. One could perhaps see workshops and classes as shorter versions of the artist-in-residence experience – an experience about not only the art work itself but the artist.

All have proved a singularly successful way of bridging the gap between the public and contemporary art

through the artist her- or himself. Art is, after all, by and about people – and the art of creation. The chance to share in that creativity is an opportunity for understanding.

Children's classes, linked to current exhibitions, have had a similar effect – and not only for the children who are encouraged to explore the contemporary work on display. The Seagate Gallery in Dundee which has run a highly successful programme for children, has found that, as spin-off to their value for youngsters, adults have discovered their own approaches to contemporary art through children's eyes. And at the same time, attendances have grown as mothers, fathers, uncles and aunts come to see what the younger members of their families have been up to.

A number of galleries have begun to use outreach programmes as a way of extending their work to a wider public – satellite exhibitions in non-professional venues – in schools, community centres, even swimming pools. Or by operating travelling galleries as they do in Fife and Aberdeen, Dumfries and Angus – and indeed as the Scottish Arts Council does with its own travelling gallery which has undertaken a highly successful series of tours, in close co-operation with local authorities.

Video can be used not only as the most contemporary art form in its own right but also as a very contemporary docent in a syle with which audiences are familiar. Indeed, video can affect more than just the public. At Kirkcaldy where the Arts Council was presenting its touring Graham Sutherland show, the gallery attendants watched the works being unpacked with little enthusiasm. Soon, however, they noticed that there was a video programme relating to the show. After watching it, they emerged far more enthusiastic. 'This guy must be good – he's been on the telly'.

The presentation of performance art has proved another successful way to draw a new public into a gallery. A recent tour by Living Artists to An Lanntair in Stornoway, Artspace in Aberdeen and the Seagate Gallery broke all attendance records. At 9 o'clock on a Sunday morning, there was a queue outside the Seagate Gallery waiting for the doors to open. Not only was the exhibition great fun but it also gave the public an enjoyable insight into an art form of which they are often suspicious. And interestingly enough the attendances at all three galleries have remained at higher level since the Living Artists show.

It's all very well doing all these things but they have also to be promoted not only in themselves but as part of the overall marketing strategy of marketing the museum itself – particularly when looking at drawing in a wider public. This, of course, is another – and, in itself, enormous topic – but it is one to which we are all needing to address ourselves and on which the Scottish Arts Council has been placing increased emphasis – indeed we have just published this handbook – Marketing the Visual Arts – which we hope will provide a useful guide for galleries and promoters of the visual arts throughout Britain.

Certainly, some museums will have problems in implementing these: low budgets, staff shortages, the demands of the existing collection, the building and its facilities etc. But if the vision exists at a senior level these can be overcome. The Scottish Arts Council has a number of schemes to help local authority museums and galleries develop their role in presenting contemporary art and the Art Department would be happy to discuss how we might help any museum which wishes to do more in this area.

I've concentrated in this paper on contemporary art rather than the contemporary arts.

But museums and galleries, of course, offer equally exciting opportunities to represent a wide range of contemporary arts – and many take advantage of their facilities and their available resources to do just that. Often such activities could be linked to exhibitions, through film, music, drama or dance. Sometimes they stand on their own right. Let's take music as an example. Many will remember the highly successful series of concerts that Colin Thompson and Leonard Friedman organised at the National Gallery of Scotland in Edinburgh. The Scottish Early Music Consort has given very popular concerts at the Burrell, while the Scottish Chamber Orchestra has not only used the Burrell for its Piccolo Pack children's concerts but the lecture theatre of the Royal Museum of Scotland too. At Aberdeen (Aberdeen again!), the attached Cowdray Hall is regularly used for concerts while there have also been chamber concerts in the gallery itself.

Galleries and museums will, I believe, find many arts organisations both open to ideas and enthusiastic about exploring possibilities. And a fresh and interesting approach to the presentation of the arts, and indeed their inter-relationship, can make tempting packages for sponsorship and for new marketing initiatives.

And in the rapidly changing background against which we all work – a new world of incentive funding, of challenges, plural economies and self-reliance – all this will I'm sure be increasingly important to us all.

We live in challenging times – but we can already see a number of Scottish galleries and museums rising to meet the new opportunities. They have set examples for others to follow. No one can belittle the task but I believe it is one well-worth pursuing as we move towards the 21st century.

G.B. Piranesi. Prison from I. Carceri c. 1761.

Museums and Scholarship

Martin Kemp

Martin Kemp is Professor of Fine Arts at the University of St. Andrews. Since 1983 he has been Associate Dean of Graduate Studies, Faculty of Arts and a Trustee of the National Galleries of Scotland, and is a Trustee of the Victoria and Albert Museum.

I am sure that there was a purpose behind the choice of cover illustration for the Museums and Galleries Commission Report on *Museum Professional Training and Career Structure* (the Hale Report). It shows one of Piranesi's great etchings of *I Carceri* – 'the Prisons'. Piranesi's awesome images of vastly incomprehensible spaces, staircases spiralling to nowhere, ramps severed in mid air, official instruments of torture and scattered remnants of lost humanity seem symbolically too close to the situation within our major museums and institutions of higher education to be funny.

In some respects the situation of curators in museums and lecturers in universities is analogous, in that both kinds of institution are subject to a series of political, economic and social pressures from which they have decreasing levels of insulation. It might be expected that these pressures would lead curators and lecturers towards common stances, and, indeed, towards shared interests and actions. However, in reality, I think it is truer to say that the different reactions to the pressures in the two kinds of institution, together with separate internal directions of development, have resulted in the professional and intellectual concerns of curators and lecturers becoming increasingly divergent. I do not think this is a desirable development, and in this paper I will be attempting to provide some degree of explanation, and suggest some possible remedies.

Any topic concerned with museums as a whole inevitably runs hard against the problem that museums and their staffing resist ready generalisation. We are faced with an enormously wide range of organisations and structures, from the equivalent of a single prison cell beside a small-town police station to enormous *carceri* like the British Museum and Victoria and Albert Museum which make Piranesi's structures seem the very soul of structural rationalism. The Commission's report makes what seems to be an obvious distinction between activities in different types of museum. In most museums – typically those under local authority management – the curators cannot develop primarily as academic specialists but need to become jacks-of-all-trades, from identifying electrotype reproductions of Renaissance medals to blue-tacking labels on walls and positioning plastic buckets under leaking roofs. However,

'an exception may be made for some staff in the great national collections and certain other highly specialised museums where the overriding purpose of the institution or department is to act as the spearhead for academic and scientific research and publication in a particular field. Staff in such institutions, particularly at more senior levels, are not necessarily responsible for the broad range of curatorial duties which occupy curatorial staff in most local museums, although they may include the words "curator" or "keeper" in their titles.'

There is an element of truth in this distinction, but I do not think it should be overplayed. Even in the most humble of local museums an object cannot be presented meaningfully to the public or given the proper care and conservation unless it is known what the object is. This knowledge involves research at one level or another. Equally, I think few curators in large national institutions these days would be able to claim in practice that they are operating *primarily* as researchers or scholars in the day-to-day run of their job. Therefore, although my remarks will be particularly orientated towards the national collections and large-scale local authority galleries, they should apply at least to some degree to all museums.

Common pressures: diverse reactions

The common factors in museums and universities are clear enough:

* operation within rigid cash limits which represent cuts in real terms (though I have to say that Universities have been treated with far greater severity in this respect);
* the dilemma that realistic salary awards and proper career structures result in loss of posts and curtailed operating budgets;
* the pressure to spend more and more time saying what one has done, is doing and will do, rather than actually doing it;

* the demand to be more managerially-minded and to be seen engaged on management activities;
* the compunction to be more commercially-orientated, raising funds through sponsorship, selling of services or marketing of products;
* and the pressure to rationalise, centralise and standardise rather than catering for creative diversity.

The list is obviously far from exhaustive, but does give a general idea of the tendencies in both kinds of institution that lead inexorably in the direction of more administration, watching and being watched, and to less time not only for research but also for simply keeping abreast of developments in the field.

Yet for all the common pressures and common effects, the reactions of the institutions has been very different. In museums, the public services aspects have grown remorselessly, particularly the mounting of glamorous exhibitions, while in universities it is the community-orientated activities that have been in the front line of cuts. I do not need to remind the reader of the findings of the Museums and Galleries Commission's Report on Museums in Scotland that the situation of university museums is truly dire. When universities have insufficient funds to safeguard what they regard as their central functions of teaching and research, the running of museums, arts centres and so on is inevitably regarded as a marginal activity with a low claim on the central budget. In the words of one Principal, 'the University can no longer act as a patron of the arts for the community'.

Under pressure, the functions and priorities of museums and universities have become more starkly differentiated. In the area of the arts, this functional differentiation has been reinforced by a range of internal intellectual developments in the institutions of higher learning that have lead away from the kinds of skills required in museums. This latter factor I will be describing in a subsequent section of this paper.

The way I intend to proceed is first to look at the situation of scholarship within museums, basing my remarks on my experience as an erstwhile Trustee of the National Galleries of Scotland and continuing Trustee of the Victoria and Albert Museum; secondly to take a view from the university stance; and finally to suggest some bridging mechanisms.

Scholarship in Museums

Scholarship now occupies a smaller amount of time in a curator's duties than in the past, and it occupies a decreasing role in the total spectrum of the activities of a museum. I should be surprised to find any professional curator dissenting from these views.

Scholarship on display at the Aberdeen University Anthropological Museum.

University of Aberdeen.

Quantification is of course difficult, as it is to say at what level the proportion of time devoted to research becomes unacceptably low. However, the Hale Report does provide some rough measures of the proportion of staff whose perceived function includes a certain degree of research and scholarship.

The museums surveyed for the report employed 812 members of staff. Only 200 of those fell into a curatorial category, while a considerable 140 were employed in administration or administrative support. Comparative percentages are provided generally for national and local authority museums – and very surprising they appear at first sight. In national museums, a meagre 9.9% of staff are employed as curators and a massive 19.9% for administration and administrative support, while in local authority museums an apparently creditable 19.6% are employed as curators. The main explanation for this disparity is that curators in local authority museums are expected to perform duties of an administrative and technical nature such as are assigned to specialist staff in the large nationals. These figures – however they are read and qualified – do present a picture of museums as service organisations in which the 'business' of running the organisation, both internally and front-of-house, has become paramount, and in which scholarship has become a less than central issue. That many members of staff remain well-informed in specialist areas, and a few are recognised as outstanding authorities on their subject – particularly in areas lying outside the curriculums of universities and polytechnics – is a tribute to the willingness of staff to spend hours of 'private' time pursuing their interests. However, the standards of scholarship, judged by the very highest ideals of the great cataloguers of the past, have undoubtedly declined.

A curator's scholarship now quite frequently consists of a rapid trawl of the most obvious literature for information on objects being assembled for a glamorous exhibition. In a few cases, particularly the specialised, in-house exhibitions, centred upon the exploration of some little-ventilated section of the museum's own collection, the scholarship may add genuine increments to the body of humane knowledge, and may even mark a conceptual shift which alters scholarly and public perceptions. We still occasionally witness the publication of a catalogue of a permanent collection, providing the definitive point of reference for anyone who subsequently wishes to enquire into the objects and make comparative reference to related items elsewhere – though the logistics and economics of producing such catalogues become progressively less favourable.

Few curators have the opportunity to undertake the life-long immersion in the primary sources, visual and documentary, that characterised the great scholar-curators of the past. Any curator who insists on a single-minded dedication to the research and exposition of objects is hardly likely to endear himself or herself to those who determine the career progress of staff in museums. The two most outstandingly single-minded scholars in the two institutions with which I have been involved have been categorised in official terms as 'difficult'. One has been shunted round various posts in the hope that his eccentricities as an administrator would do least conspicuous damage, while the other faces a future of blocked career propects and being marginalised in the formation of policy.

The problems arise partly from generalised social factors, – embraced conveniently under the term the 'leisure industries', – and more directly from conscious policy. The whole thrust in the recent management of museums has been to emphasise the mechanisms of management over the individual and collective creativity of the staff with respect to the objects. The catch-phrase has been 'the management must be allowed to manage' – a reasonable enough proposition on the face of it, but a rule which can be used to justify unrestrained mis-management as readily as it may be used to promote efficient and humane teamwork. I should say, in this context, that the present composition of the Trustee Boards of our national museums must bear substantial responsibility for structures by which the Board only hears what it wants to hear, and even then only within the limits of what the Director decides it should hear. The Boards in general do not seem to be fully representative either of the community as a whole or of the main consumers of the museum, including the world of education and scholarship. Trustee Boards, as recently composed, have become increasingly unresponsive to the main body of people employed in the organisation, not least to the senior scholars. In these circumstances, it is not surprising that even senior curators feel remote from the decision-making process and that the back-room activity of scholarship on which scholarly publications are founded has an inconspicuous profile for the governing boards.

The View from the Universities

In that high-level activity in art history gains considerable support from the general public interest in art of the past, the scholarly work of lecturers in higher education and of staff in museums may be regarded as integral parts of the 'arts industry' as a whole. The relationship between scholarly activities and the public face of the 'museums business' is clearly symbiotic, in that all exhibitions and publications aimed at other than an entirely specialist audience contribute to the enormous heightening of public interest in the visual arts – apparent in the last 30 years or so and continuing today. I think the same is true, perhaps to a lesser extent, in other areas of museum and academic activity, though it does appear that history of science as a whole has a less developed public and academic structure than its inherent importance might lead us to expect.

This upsurge in activity in the arts industry is at least in part a result of the proselytising efforts of museums, scholars and the media in general, while it in turn inspires successively more people with the desire to pursue formal studies in the area. University, polytechnic or college graduates across the range of arts and sciences provide a large proportion of the regular consumers of art in museums and exhibitions. An increasing number of graduates have experienced some formal exposure to art history at some point of their careers, and increasing numbers are graduating with a qualification in the subject.

In addition to this general symbiosis between museums and those who have experienced higher education, there is of course the more specific relationship in the case of museum staff who have received a tertiary education. Of the 200 curators in Hale's survey group, 199 possessed first degrees, 43 higher degrees by research, 51 postgraduate qualifications through taught courses, and 24 were products of the Manchester and Leicester University postgraduate museum courses. The possession of a specific vocational qualification on entry into the profession is still the exception rather than the rule, and the majority of staff enter with an academic qualification founded upon traditional scholarly pursuits. Most of the staff subsequently need to learn the job.

I think it is true to say, in art history at least, that the curriculums of the increasingly numerous degree courses in Britain have tended to move away from rather than towards the object-based skills typical of museum scholarship. Most courses pay lip-service to the need to study works of art in the original, and most arrange study visits to museums for this purpose, but I do not consider that these activities can claim to inculcate object-based or museological skills in any profound sense. The Hale Report saw few signs of the teaching of specifically museum-orientated skills in first degree courses. The reasons for the general divorce of academic art history and museums are both intellectual and practical.

The intellectual reasons concern the strong trend in academic art history away from attribution, dating, stylistic and technical analysis and towards such questions as patronage, theory, iconography, semiotics, methodology and social history. In such varieties of history the object tends to become illustrative of a context rather than the particularised focus of attention as the means and ends of the enquiry. In looking at the most fashionable trends in art history, it is difficult to think of any museum-based historian who is producing publications which are essential reading for anyone who wishes to keep abreast of the latest approaches. This stands in marked contrast to the last century and the earlier stages of this century, when many of the epoch-making publications originated with staff working in museums. The museum is not a natural home for many of the new varieties of art history, though there are signs that some curators of collections of fine and applied arts may be sufficiently affected by the new ideas to attempt the redisplay of their collections as illustrative of social history. In most instances, this does not seem to me to be the best or most appropriate use of the visual material in museums, particularly if it results in each object becoming subsumed insignificantly within a cosmetic reconstruction or a picturesque past in which polystyrene plays a more conspicuous role than pictures or pots.

The practical reasons for the separation are all the result of growth: the growth of burdens of professional and bureaucratic duties in both museums and universities etc, which mean that individual staff find less and less time for co-operative ventures lying outside their specific 'job description'; and the growth in student numbers, which means that even a single honours topic in one university department can attract more students than can be feasibly handled in a behind-the-scenes visit to a museum. A spectacular symptom of this pressure is the Tate Gallery now forbidding access for undergraduates to its archival holdings, even for those students writing dissertations on British art. Even

The history of the university at the Hunterian Museum, University of Glasgow.
Hunterian Museum, University of Glasgow.

at the level of postgraduate or staff research the pressure of numbers can have serious consequences, as witnessed by the inability of many photographic services (most notably the British Museum) to supply photographs within a reasonable period.

I should say that in my personal experience I have experienced nothing but the greatest willingness on the part of curators to aid the research and study of their collections. But translating this willingness into specific action in which museums and teaching institutions come together in co-operative ventures relies as always upon the initiatives of the individuals involved – and I have already stressed that the increasing professional demands upon staff within their own institutions discourages such initiatives. As an example, I can cite the excellent series of university seminars initiated by the National Galleries of Scotland and the Scottish Universities, a scheme which subsequently extended to Glasgow Art Gallery, the Hunterian Museum and, on one occasion, to a privately-owned house. A series of topics were chosen, each designed to focus interest upon a particularly strong aspect of each gallery's holdings and to draw substantially upon museum-based skills in curation and conservation. After running very successfully for a number of years, the series seems to have fallen into abeyance. The departure and non-replacement of the Keeper of Education at the National Galleries did not help. Ultimately the organisational burden fell on the same few willing individuals year after year, and, in the absence of any formal procedure by which the series was automatically continued, the impetus gradually diminished for the want of others to take up the organisational commitment. It all takes time and effort – and there is not much of either to spare in our professional lives at present.

Some Suggestions

The Hale Report recognised two areas for action: the provision of museum-orientated skills in educational courses at undergraduate and postgraduate levels; and the freeing of the ossified career structures and broadening of intellectual opportunities for staff in museums. My suggestions relate the way in which scholarship in museums and universities can be brought together in such a way as to assist progress in those two areas.

The Report (3.19b) encourages the practice of museum personnel lecturing in universities, but the practical problems – lack of funds even for meeting lecturer's travel costs, and a natural reluctance to impose upon the services of the same lecturer year after year – mean that this can play only a very minor role in any interchange of skills. Ultimately I think the only substantial way to proceed is for the movement of personnel from one type of institution to another. There is no prospect of large-scale career movements from the museum to the lecturing profession and *vice versa*, and it therefore follows that short-term exchanges are the only practical answer.

At the training level this would imply some kind of internship system, whereby a museum department would take in a student for a fixed period of between three and twelve months to undertake a programme of studies in museum skills. It would need to be accepted that such an internship would not produce fully-fledged curators, but it would provide the student with an awareness of the nature of the tasks encountered in museums, and some ideas as to how the duties can be performed.

The two-year postgraduate M.Litt. courses at St. Andrews in Gallery Studies and National Trust for Scotland Studies, in which the student's second year is devoted to the preparation of a thesis on some aspects of the collection or activities of the host institution, provides some idea of the possibilities and the problems. During the four years of its operation the course has proved popular with applicants (in spite of a deliberately low publicity profile), has resulted in a series of theses of considerable quality, and has to date an encouraging record in graduate employment. However, the practical problems have been considerable.

1) the students have found it almost impossible to obtain grant funding, having to compete for major postgraduate awards with all kinds of research students in all arts subjects;
2) the instruction of students within the university

has to be squeezed out of already over-worked schedules, with no special resourcing in teaching time, library and other materials;

3) the arrangement with each host institution in the second year is of an *ad hoc* nature, and is dependent on the relevant member(s) of staff being willing and having the time to play a role in the design, research and production of the thesis. The student is not physically 'based' in the museum or gallery, and some of the museums have very limited study facilities in which the student can work 'on site'.

I think there is a strong case for the scheme to be extended by a series of formal internships (as recommended by Hale 3.19.b) in Scottish museums, but these would need to be properly resourced as Hale stresses. In the context of the St. Andrews course, I would see the internships as greatly enhancing the vocational element without losing the distinctive academic strength of the qualification as a master's degree with a substantial research component. The research would continue to be devoted particularly to topics (eg. metal work or textiles) for which little academic instruction is normally available in universities.

My second suggestion is similarly related to an existing initiative. The National Museums of Scotland and University of St. Andrews successfully applied to the Leverhulme Trust for the financing of the first-ever joint research held jointly within a museum and a university department. The appointee, Howard Coutts from the Victoria and Albert Museum, has recently commenced on a three-year programme of research, teaching and publication in the field of ceramic decoration. The advantages of the fellowship are:

1) to achieve a piece of sustained research in a particularly rich aspect of the museum's collection and to publish the results of the research in both specialist and publically-accessible forms;

2) to permit someone who already possesses (or is willing to develop) object-based skills, and who would find little opportunity for sustained research if employed in regular curatorial duties, to undertake fundamental thought and research in a particular area;

3) to place someone with object-based skills in a university context, whereby interested students can be provided with an insight into these skills in a way normally unavailable to them;

4) to encourage a general dialogue between university-based and museum-based scholarship.

It is too early to assess the results, but I am already confident that it is a worthwhile initiative which could be extended on a wider basis. The Hale Report recognises the lack of opportunities for career development in museums, in both administrative and academic areas. I should like to suggest that a regular museum fellowship should be established for a curator to work for a period on attachment in a university. There may also be the possibility of movement in the other direction, with lecturers spending a period on secondment in a museum. For practical reasons it is difficult to see a lecturer effectively assuming a full range of curatorial duties on a short-term secondment, but the educational service of a museum might provide a natural home for a lecturer. There would also be the exciting possibility of a scholar working on secondment on a catalogue in a particular area of the collections which may lie outside the special expertise of the existing gallery staff.

The kind of standing fellowships I am envisaging will also require resourcing – the Leverhulme grant is for this one specific fellowship – but I think that a great deal of good could be accomplished over the years on a cumulative basis at a relatively minute cost in relation to the total cost of the museum services to the state. The transfusing of ideas and skills between museums and scholars outside museums can only be accomplished through individual adventure and flexibility – but it requires institutional structures and initiatives to provide the context for that flexibility. Left to their own devices, the structures will (as we can already see) become more insulated from each other rather than more closely related. Such progressive separation is something that should be actively resisted for the good of both 'sides'.

But does all this matter beyond a narrow range of professional concerns? Is it of any relevance to the great body of visitors, who clearly lie at the heart of the topics covered in other papers in the present volume?

I would argue that all the expectations harboured by the public have their ultimate roots in basic research. It is basic research that has reorientated our appreciation of Victorian art and architecture. It is basic research that has taught us to read artefacts from a social standpoint. It is basic research that has developed awareness of our great industrial heritage – and so on. If we neglect the research base, we will create a climate which precludes the conceptual shifts that permit our historic heritage to play a living role in the present. An image of museums which limits them to responding to known public demand is far too passive, static and uncreative. I believe passionately that scholarship at the highest level is vital if museums are actively to play the creative and educative role which lies at the heart of their value to society.

Two members of Northam First School interview Harry Triggs as part of Southampton City Museum's Northam and Chapel Oral History Project.

Dave Roberts, Southampton City Museums.

Museums in Education

Eilean Hooper-Greenhill

Eilean Hooper-Greenhill joined the Department of
Museum Studies at the University of Leicester as
Lecturer in 1980, having previously been
Education Officer at the National Portrait Gallery
in London. She has published widely on museums
and education.

1. Introduction

Now is the time when many museums are seeking to
build bridges of many sorts with other organizations,
institutions and groups. At a time of new aspirations, it
is always profitable to use the existing expertise, and
the skills that have already been developed. The
educational workers of the museum have always needed
the involvement of other organizations and have
worked from a number of fundamental premises that
may now be of interest to other museum workers. This
paper sets out to discuss the nature of education in the
museum, to identify the operational and philosophical
premises on which links with other organizations are
based, and to provide examples of their application.

2. The Nature of Museum Education

Firstly we should be very clear what we mean by
museum education. The museum is an institution that
can offer an educational experience across a wide range
of variables and in relation to a wide range of
institutions and organizations. For a long time working
with other organizations was limited to work with
formal educational provision at all levels. But
increasingly museums are relating their educational
work to concepts drawn from life-long learning.[1]

Life-long learning works with the premise that people
learn throughout their lives and not only as children in
formal educational arrangements. Learning takes place
in other places and from other people. Life-long learning
recognises that the need to learn may be directly
related to the current life-experiences of the individual,
and that therefore different needs manifest themselves
at different times throughout life. Learning experiences
are devised that are 'student centred', enabling the
learner to proceed at their own pace, and to identify
and develop their own interests. The 'learner' is seen as
an active maker of his/her own learning experiences,
with the 'teacher' acting as facilitator in this process. Of
course, part of the role of the facilitator is to devise an
appropriate structure that provides support when the
learner requires it, but which enables a variety of forms
of engagement with this support. In most museums the
potential for educational provision is so enormous that
there is no difficulty selecting and enabling educational
experiences, even for groups coming from formal
institutions, that have many of the desirable qualities of
life-long learning.

The value of working with museums includes the opportunity to encounter real things, which without a doubt have strong educational potential simply because they are real. There is the potential of putting reading and learning from secondary sources into a material context. The use of drama, artists/craftsmen, or historical demonstrations, offers the possibility of meeting and learning from 'real' people. Learning can be facilitated through the use of narrative, or problem-solving, to suit age or ability. Education in the museum can be slanted towards the development of skills, skills of observation, documentation, recording, analysis, detection of bias, extraction of information. Learning in groups and through discussion is particularly appropriate.

One of the great possibilities of museum education is that it enables the teaching of thinking.[2] It enables the development of critical faculties, of rational argument, of deductive learning. By working with real things, making comparisons, remembering, making relationships, interrogating, moving from concrete observations to abstract concepts, moving from specific observations to generalisations, extending from the known to the unknown, following the pace and the interests of the learner, true cognitive and emotional processes may take place that lead to changed perceptions and the growth of new ideas.[3]

Much of the educational potential of the museum is close to the sort of educational experience that *ought* to emerge from the new government directives over Standard Grade and GCSE. The type of experience that the new curricula suggest entails giving learners the experience, skills, and knowledge that should enable them to think clearly, to act appropriately, and to sustain effort in such a way that their long-term life-potential and specific immediate opportunities are both maximised. The new examination initiatives require methods that relate closely to the existing methods of museum education and consequently opportunities

exist to draw museum education into the mainstream educational world in a new way. Several new initiatives are at the preliminary stages of investigating methods of resource-based learning and new training programmes for teachers are also beginning to make their appearance.

Other aspects of government planning are difficult to assess at this stage, but many aspects are worrying. The content of the national curriculum in England and Wales will be laid down centrally, which may well mean less autonomy for teachers in planning whether or not to include museum visits as part of their teaching. The planned tests at 7, 11, 14, and 16 seem likely to demand a style and content of teaching that will not encourage discovery or learner-centred methods, and thus will not encourage out of school learning. The fundamental changes in school organization are going to lead to confusion on many levels at least in the short term, which is again inhibiting in relation to the development of new teaching methods. What does seem apparent is that teachers are going to need to be very clear indeed about their objectives in relation to museum use, and that museums are going to have to develop forms of co-operation that encourage both clear thinking and a variety of different forms of engagement with collections, displays, and archival material. This will require the museum to identify firstly the different potential experiences that they can offer, and then secondly, to develop relevant communication strategies. In a transitional and complex situation, the museum will need to be seen to be very clear-sighted and steady.

In relation to the links that it is possible for museums to make with other organizations from the museums' point of view, the 'possible' is enabled by the 'paid for'. Funding arrangements for educational provision in museums have always been complex and a variety of situations exist where many different arrangements apply.[4] However, funding is critical in relation to who may work with whom. Seconded teachers, and those directly funded through the local education authority, tend to work exclusively with schoolchildren and teachers. Education officers, funded through the museum budget, are freer to work with other groups and organizations apart from schools. Some appointments are made specifically with links into the broader community in mind. There is an interesting new initiative in Dundee, where a trainee post, based in the personnel department of the local District Council is attached to the museum service's department of the extension services. The post-holder is at the same time studying for a postgraduate qualification in Community Education at Dundee College of Education. 'Section Eleven' posts, (Local Government Act 1966) with funding from central government in relation to special provision for ethnic groups, have enabled the appointment in England of officers specifically working with groups and organizations from different ethnic communities.

New funding is being actively sought by education staff to extend their ways of working. At Norwich, a writer in residence was funded with cooperation from the Eastern Arts Association Visiting Writers Scheme, where the museum paid the writer's expenses and Eastern Arts paid the fee. At Dulwich College Picture Gallery in London a writer, an artist and a scientist are currently in residence for a term each, funded through business sponsorship. The Manpower Services Commission has provided funds for the educational work of museums as it has for other areas of museum work, and some examples will be discussed below.

3. Basic educational principles

Educational workers have always followed some basic operational principles in order to ensure the validity of their work: after all, an education service with no customers fails conspicuously.

1. Not everyone comes to work with the museum for the same reason, and sometimes it is not very clear why people might wish to be involved. What are the needs and expectations of the groups that the museum will work with? The same programme or provision is not appropriate for both seven-year olds and old age pensioners. The expectations of the group must be identified if they are to be fulfilled. The different expectations, interests and experiences of the groups to be served will alter the nature of the provision, even though the same theme, or the same objects may be used on each occasion.

2. The visit to the museum does not take place in a vacuum. What is the use to which the museum experience is to be put? What happens before and after the museum visit? In other words, what is the context of the work to be done in the museum?

3. It is recognized that working with the museum is not easy. What support should be provided for the visiting groups? Do the group leaders need introductory courses in the museum about the museum collections, or about how to use objects? Do they need materials to be studied at home or at school and if so what? Do they need bibliographies in relation to the things to be studied, or slides, or loan boxes? Would visits by museum workers to their own bases be helpful, either before or after the work in the museum?

4. Educational work requires a specific expertise. In general this work is carried out by trained people who know about the context from which groups come, and who can relate to them on their own terms. Equally, it is recognized that group leaders are also likely to be experts in their own fields. Working with groups from special education, for example, generally requires the museum staff to acknowledge and learn from the teachers who have this very specific experience and training. Thus the museum/user-organization relationship is one based on mutual respect and

acknowledgement of skills and experience. I want to stress this because many of the failed relationships that I have observed in museums have been due to the museums failure to acknowledge and learn from the expertise of those with whom they wished to work.

5. Although it is of course necessary to develop new contacts, it is seen as desirable to strengthen existing links and to establish long-term mutually supportive relationships. One-off provision is generally regarded as less satisfactory. How can existing enthusiastic users influence future planning, how can interest and involvement be sustained?

These basic and necessary operational principles are supported by some equally fundamental and equally necessary philosophical principles.

Most museum educationalists would believe that they should make special provision for individual groups rather than a bulk provision for all, and that quality of experience was more important than quantity of groups dealt with; would want to work in relation to topics or objects from the existing experience and interests of the group, rather than from what the museum as expert thinks should be known about a particular thing; would enable growth from one experience to another; and recognizing the people learn in different ways, and at different speeds, would, as far as possible, provide many different experiences as entry points into the learning process. Most importantly, recognizing that motivation and enthusiasm is the key to successful learning, most museum educationalists would work very hard to enable success for all participants, including both members and leaders of groups, on their own terms.[5]

These operational and philosophical principles lie behind the educational work of the museum in their relationships with other organizations. I will go on to describe some examples as illustrations.

4. Examples

The Education Centre at the Horniman Museum in South London has been well-known for valuable and qualitative educational provision for some years. The staff of the centre are on permanent secondment from the Inner London Education Authority (ILEA). Lasting links have been made over the years with the educational establishment in the ILEA. A specific project outlines the complex structural network between museum, school, inspectorate, and advisory teachers.[6]

Division 7 of the ILEA (Lewisham) chose museum education as one of its curriculum development projects in 1981. The aims of the project were extensive, including specific educational objectives and social objectives. They related to the interests of the teachers, the children, the Inspectorate and the museum. The aims were as follows: to show how the museum could be used as a resource in the primary school; to develop an interdisciplinary and cross-curricular approach to work carried out using museum objects; to help children and teachers to understand the importance of museum collections as primary evidence, and to develop skills for using the collections in learning; to use a study of objects from comparative cultures to develop positive and receptive attitudes to other cultures; to give children an enjoyable experience in the museum and thereby a positive perception of museums.

The Divisional Inspector who initiated the project held initial discussions with the three Horniman Museum teachers. Six primary schools, chosen to represent a cross-section in terms of accommodation, internal organization and catchment areas, took part in the project. An extensive pre-planning process took place, with the Horniman teachers visiting each school that was to take part, and the staff from all the schools visiting the museum. Because the project was initiated by the Inspector, some teachers were forcibly involved who would not otherwise have thought the museum a suitable place to take their children. (These teachers have now become users on a regular basis.)

Classes in each school worked for a term on the museum project, with teachers and children choosing their own topic to study based on the collections. In some cases pre-visits led to choice of topic based on the interests of the children, who voted for their preference. Twenty-three different topics were covered by children ranging in age from 4–11. All the collections of the museum were used. Forty-eight teachers were involved overall, and each class made at least one and sometimes three visits to the museum. In some schools the project was sustained for as long as a year.

The project was coordinated by the Horniman teachers, the advisory teacher for primary education in the division, and one designated teacher from each school. This group met regularly to review the progress and the visits. The six head teachers involved also met regularly to monitor progress and exchange ideas. In the first term of the project seventeen after-school visits were arranged in the museum for the teachers so that the visits could be discussed, the teachers could get to know each other, the museum, and the education centre teachers. Because some teachers were initially suspicious, these visits were crucial to reassure them that the education centre staff could handle their children, and to give them the confidence required to bring 'difficult' children to the museum.

The role of the museum teachers was to introduce the museum and some of its objects and support the teachers. The bulk of the work was undertaken in the schools following up and extending the observations and ideas uncovered by the museum visit. This work extended into art, maths, environmental studies, and R E, and resulted in written work, craft work, a play and a rock musical.

The Horniman teachers went into each of the schools afterwards to see the work produced and to congratulate the staff and the children on their successes.

Each school produced an exhibition of the work done, and some work from each school was displayed in the museum. Each of the six schools wrote up a comprehensive report detailing the methods used, and describing the work undertaken. These were used to extend the work of the project. The reports were circulated to all Lewisham schools shortly after the completion of the project. Groups of head teachers from primary schools that had not been part of the project were brought into the museum to hear from one of the participating teachers and from the museum teachers. This jointly had the effect of spreading the information about the value and potential of museum education, and was effective in that many more primary schools from this area did in fact later approach the museum.

A large scale coordinated approach such as this has a number of advantages. It draws in more people, and, because it was initiated through the Inspectorate, perhaps those that might not have thought about using the museum; it opens a wider debate on method and possibilities and has a training element for both teachers and Inspectorate; it provides a support structure for participants; it results in work and written accounts that are available for others to consult.[7]

The project was successful because of the careful networks that were built up, the many levels of pre-planning and evaluation that were integral to the project, and because the needs of all the various participants were considered.

I want to describe now a group of projects with non-school organizations that demonstrate different ways of working with objects and that raise questions in relation to the adaptablility of the museum when working with other organizations.

Help the Aged have a number of approaches to projects with old people that are of relevance to museums, and several museums have worked with them in a number of ways. Help the Aged's Education and Research Department have produced 'Recall' and 'Reminiscence' materials which encourage older people to remember and share memories about their experiences. These materials generally take the form of slides and photographs, and tapes of music and comments. These materials are well complemented by some museum objects, particularly those that relate to the early part of this century.

Using concrete objects is an easy way into talking and remembering. Talking in itself enables the expression of ideas and the formation of concepts, the expression of feelings to others, all exercises in communication. For some elderly people this alone can be valuable. Their experiences and opinions are seen to be of value simply because someone is listening. Observation, interpretation, analysis, comparison, classification, are all valuable cognitive exercises that are increasingly being recognized as good in themselves for learners of all ages. For the elderly they help to keep the brain active and to engender a sense of social worth often denied to them.

A project funded by the Manpower Services Commission (MSC) and based at Warwick Museum enabled a small team to take museum objects into day centres, hospitals and old people's homes with the aim of providing a stimulating experience for the old people through their reactions to the artefacts which were selected for their specific relevance. Help the Aged training packs were used by the museum team at the beginning of the project to raise their own awareness.

The knowledge that the elderly have to offer about objects, their use and context, can be immensely valuable to the museum. Again with MSC funding, Southampton Museum has used oral history projects not only as a form of educational outreach to contact those people who do not normally visit museums, but also in relation to mainstream curatorial activities.[8] On the grounds that most standard collecting practices, whether purchase, donation or loan, leads to the accumulation of objects that come from sectors of society already well-represented in the collections, oral history projects are being used to gain access to artefacts that would normally be lost to the museum. Working with groups such as the Co-operative Women's Guild, and unemployed groups, in the production of exhibitions, has uncovered new sources of objects. In the process of working on collaborative exhibitions the museum staff have found themselves re-evaluating their role. In working with the local community and its history, both curators and educationalists have become part of the processes of making history. The involvement of the museum staff has become much closer to that of the facilitator of experience that is the role of the teacher in life-long learning, rather than the expert with a body of knowledge to transmit, which is perhaps seen as the traditional role of museum staff.

It seems to me that this movement of the museum towards the society which it is now seen to serve is becoming more important as museums assess their social positions on the eve of the twenty-first century. And part of the shift, if it is to be towards the needs of the public, must mean a reorientation of the work of the museum. The ethical role of the museum in society is also under debate in other parts of the world.

This last summer I was working in Brazil. In a society with very great extremes of access to housing, wealth, education, and a dignified existence, the museum stands all too obviously as an institution that has vast resources, and enormous wealth, in stark contrast to the vast bulk of the population that has very few resources indeed. Following the spirit of the Round Table of Santiago de Chile[9] that came to the conclusion that in such a society the museum must put itself at the service of the community in which it exists, many of the museums in Brazil are endeavouring to move towards the people and their needs.

The Observatory Museum in Rio de Janeiro has begun to build a Science Park in its grounds. These exhibits are designed to illustrate simple scientific concepts through play, activity, and personal experiment. The exhibits themselves have undergone a rigorous process of evaluation and are at present being constructed on a permanent site in the museum. They will be used in the teaching of the many school groups that come to the Observatory for their science lessons, but the ideas are also being used in conjunction with the work of a group called Living Science Space, which consists of university lecturers, researchers, teachers and other interested parties.[10] The team from the Observatory Museum take their equipment onto the beaches of Rio and into the 'favelas', the shanty towns, to set up demonstrations and to work with the people who come to watch and join in. The exhibits are kept very simple so that they can be replicated by teachers or others. A book has been produced that describes the educational gain of the exhibits, the aims of the experiments, the scientific details and the method of construction.[11] Working with the inhabitants of the slums in Rio is forcing the museum and university workers to recognize that science is not merely 'fun' and 'exciting', which would seem to be the rationale that informs many of the new science centres that are burgeoning around the world, but that 'scientific literacy' is a necessity if people are to begin to understand how science can and does affect our lives.[12]

The National Fine Art Museum in Rio is also concerned to contribute what it can to help the 'children of the street'. The education department works with a benevolent society, the Sociedade Benficente Sao Martinho, which works to help the children that live permanently on the streets in Rio. The aims of the society are to help the children to achieve more dignified lives, to help them gain educational and work experience, and to give them access to health and care. The museum runs art programmes to introduce them to both ideas and practical work, and has also introduced the children to the museum as a workplace.[13] Two of the youngsters who have been connected with the museum for a number of years are now working in the museum as electricians.

In Sao Paulo, the Museu Lasar Segall, a small art gallery in the house of the artist Segall, has found ways of employing one or two of these underprivileged young people. In order to enable them to participate in a meaningful way in the museum, radical new management processes are used that, in effect, train the museum workers in decision-making and public speaking. The museum is, in one sense, supplying the civic education that these young people have been denied, using itself as an ongoing practical learning base.

5. Conclusions

Working with other organizations means seeing things from other points of view. In the past many museums have been very bad indeed at this and some conspicuous failures can be logged.

If museums want to work with other organizations in the future, I think some lessons must be learnt and some critical reviews of practice must be undertaken.

Needs and expectations on both parts must be identified. A mutual set of aims, objectives, and obligations must be specified. If the expectations and the demands are too high, and the museum does not expect to be able to produce the resources, the collaboration must not be undertaken because it will lead to failure and disillusionment on the part of both collaborating organizations. Evaluation of the work at Southampton has demonstrated that negative impressions of the museum are easily achieved through lack of commitment and lack of sustained funding,[14] and how often does one hear museum staff complaining about the inabilities and idiocies of the groups they have been working with?

Time and resources must be made available. Successful collaboration demands much planning and continuous evaluation from the point of view of all the collaborators. The example from the Horniman Museum demonstrated a sensitive and elaborate evaluation strategy. If something like this, that at least begins to ask what the experience means to the participating organizations, is not established, I think the museum can be accused of abusing the goodwill of collaborators. Perhaps this sensitivity is particularly acute in relation to the educational work of the museum, but if this sort of collaborative working is to extend to the production of exhibitions and to collecting processes in museums, then this quality of care and thought is necessary here too.

In conclusion, if museums are to collaborate successfully with other organizations, we must be prepared to consider the needs of others, which may mean adapting our own, we must be open-minded and prepared to see things from other points of view, and we must be willing to get involved in serious commitments rather than token one-off events. This will involve a lot of hard work, but in the end, must be the way forward.

References

[1] Cropley, A.J.   *Towards a system of life long education;* Unesco and Pergamon Press, 1980; Millas, J.G. 'Museums and life long education', *Museum*, 25(3), 1973, pp. 157-164.

[2] Delahaye, M.   'Can children be taught to think?' *The Listener* 22 October, 1987, p. 14.

[3] Henningar-Shuh, J.   'Teaching yourself to teach with objects', *Journal of Education* 7(4) n.d. Nova Scotia, Canada. The permission of the author has been given to make copies of this article available through the Department of Museum Studies, University of Leicester.

[4] Bateman, J.   'The control and funding of museum education services in Britain', *Museums Journal* 84(2), 1984, pp. 51-55.

[5] For a further discussion of museum education see Ambrose, T. (ed.) *Education in Museums; Museums in Education*, Scottish Museums Council, HMSO, Edinburgh, 1987.

[6] Mellors, M.   'Horniman Museum and Primary Schools', *Journal of Education in Museums*, 3, 1982, p. 19.

[7] These reports are held by Mary Mellors at the Horniman Museum, who may be able to make copies available. A set is also held in the Department of Museum Studies, University of Leicester, where they may be consulted.

[8] Jones, S. and Major, C.   'Reaching the public: oral history as a survival strategy for museums', *Oral History Journal* 12(2), 1986, pp. 31-38.

[9] Terrugi, M.E.   'The Round Table of Santiago, Chile', *Museum*, 25(3), 1973, pp. 128-133.

[10] Bazin, M.   'Three years of living science: learning from experience'. *Scientific Literacy Papers,* University of Oxford, Department for External Studies, 1987.

[11] Schvarsberg, B. *et al.   Parque da Ciencia: o brinquedo como possibilidade do aprendizado,* Museu de Astronomia e Ciencias Afins/CNPq, Rio de Janeiro, Brazil, 1987.

[12] Shortland, M.   'No business like show business', *Nature* 328, 16th July, 1987, p. 213.

[13] *Projeto alternativas de atendimento aos meninos de rua*, projeto Museu Nacional de Belas Artes, Extra Muros, Meninos de rua, Oficina de arte, Rio de Janeiro, 1985.

[14] Jones and Major, *op. cit.* note 8, p. 37.

Many thanks to Mary Mellors, Sian Jones, Margaret Wood, Grant Ogilvie and Adam Ritchie for their help in supplying information for this paper.

Part 2
Museums working with Museums

Young visitors at a pottery workshop, part of a Leisure Learning Programme at Alloa Museum organized with help from the Scottish Museums Council. The programme was based on a touring exhibition 'Susie Cooper Pottery.'

Alloa Advertiser.

Area Museum Councils in the United Kingdom: the benefits

Chris Newbery

Chris Newbery has been Deputy Secretary of the
Museums and Galleries Commission since 1985.
He has previously held appointments as the first
London Museums Officer for the Area Museum
Service for South Eastern England and as Curator
of Newport Museum and Art Gallery in Gwent.

Introduction

For the majority of staff working in the non-national
museum sector it is difficult to imagine life without the
Area Museum Councils (AMCs). The *Review of Area
Museum Councils and Services* published by the Museums
and Galleries Commission (MGC) in 1984 broadly
concurred with the view expressed by one supplier of
evidence that 'Area Museum Services are the most
important and worthwhile development that the
museum profession has enjoyed in its history.' Yet the
first Area Museum Council was established less than
thirty years ago in the South West of England. There are
now nine Area Museum Councils; seven for England and
one each for Scotland and Wales. An Area Museum
Council for Northern Ireland has been recommended by
the MGC and it is hoped that the Government will find
the resources to establish one in the not-too-distant
future.

So what is an Area Museum Council? As defined in the
MGC's *Review of Area Museum Councils and Services*,
essentially it is a membership organisation consisting of
representatives of museums and the organisations
which run them, with the objective of helping non-
national (local) museums to improve the standards of
care for their collections and service to the public. This
is done by fostering and increasing co-operation,
providing common services and information and
distributing government funds to approved projects.
Area Museum Councils are not statutory bodies; their
provision is the result of voluntary agreements by their
members. With one exception, they are all now
incorporated under the Companies Acts and registered
as Charities. The seven English Area Museum Councils
receive a substantial part of their funding from central
government, channelled through the MGC, while those
in Scotland and Wales receive theirs direct through the
Scottish and Welsh Offices.

Although the level of central government support for Area Museum Councils has risen from £10,000 in 1963/64 to over £3 million in 1987/88, the number of museums in the UK has also increased dramatically during that period to over 2,000. Our knowledge of the technical requirements necessary for the long-term preservation of museum collections has also increased, while the public demand for better interpretation of collections has led to greater pressure on available resources.

The MGC's *Review of Area Museum Councils and Services* recommended nothing short of a doubling of funds in real terms over a five year period from 1985. For the last two years the MGC has only been able to pass on funding increases to English Area Museum Councils which are broadly in line with inflation. Scotland and Wales have not fared much better. The Minister for the Arts has recently announced the Museums and Galleries Commission's budget for the next three years and it is clear that the Commission will be struggling to maintain its policy of protecting English Area Museum Councils from the effects of inflation. Indeed, if one takes into account the history of local government salary awards in excess of inflation, the Area Museum Councils will be under increasing pressure to find alternative sources of funding if they wish to maintain current levels of service and grant-aid to museums. It is as well to bear this challenging financial situation in mind when reviewing the services which Area Museum Councils currently provide for their members.

Assistance to Museums

The schemes and services eligible for grant-aid from the Area Museum Councils were originally set out in a Treasury Memorandum. However, the Museums and Galleries Commission obtained grant-in-aid status in April 1987 and is in the process of formulating a revised set of guidelines. These will certainly apply to the English Area Museum Councils which are its revenue clients, but it is anticipated that the guidelines will also be adopted by the Welsh and Scottish Area Museum Councils.

The schemes and services which Area Museum Councils will be able to grant-aid or subsidise in future, fall into four broad categories: the care of collections; the interpretation of collections; the marketing of museums; and the provision of museum-related advice, information and training. As grants can only be awarded for specific projects, the funding of museum staff can only be undertaken on a pump-priming basis. With regard to the level of grant-aid, English Area Councils only have to demonstrate that grants offered to members do not exceed 50% of the total cost of all schemes helped in any one year. Given that the total gross cost of assisted schemes may amount to several £ million compared with Area Council's grant-aid budgets which range from circa £107,000 to £215,000 (1986-87), there is considerable room for flexibility. Indeed, Area Councils may offer up to 100% grants in selected cases, provided that this is compensated for by a lower precentage grant elsewhere. This flexibility is of potential benefit to the smaller, less well-off museum, which has traditionally struggled to find the matching funds under the old pound for pound system. However, the provision of block grants or other arrangements whereby individual museums are in effect guaranteed funding on a regular annual basis will not be permitted.

Whilst the new MGC spending guidelines will give Area Councils greater flexibility as to how they spend their money, overall financial constraints mean that grants will have to be targeted if they are to give maximum benefit to the recipient museums. Firstly, it is important to be clear about the eligibility of institutions for grant-aid. At the moment, each Area Council has its own membership criteria and it is possible that a museum might be acceptable in one area and not in another.

This problem should be dispensed with once the MGC's

scheme to establish a Register of Museums meeting minimum standards has been fully implemented. Briefly, the requirements will concern conformity with the Museum Association's definition of a museum; an acceptable constitution and financial status; an acceptable statement of collection management policy; and formal access to professional curatorial advice. The registration scheme is due to commence in 1988 and it is planned that the initial register should be completed within four years. Registration will not only form a 'baseline' for Area Museum Council membership; it will also enable other funding agencies to know if a museum is worthy of support as a long-term investment.

Having established that a museum is eligible for grant-aid in principle, an Area Council also needs to ensure that its money is going to be spent in a sensible manner. Increasingly, Area Councils are adopting grant policies which set out priorities for their members. In some instances their policies have been informed by needs surveys, such as the one undertaken by the North of England Area Museum Service in 1982. The Yorkshire and Humberside Museum Council grant policy for 1987/88 for example, states that 60% or more of available funds will be set aside for projects which fall within the following priority areas:

a) conservation treatment of objects;
b) environmental monitoring and control;
c) storage improvements;
d) security;
e) documentation improvements;
f) short training courses with special reference to the subjects outlined above.

In other words, Yorkshire and Humberside's money is being targeted principally towards care of collections. The policy goes on to state that the sums available for financing permanent exhibition projects will primarily be limited to schemes of very special benefit to the museum concerned or to the Area. It also says that

consideration will be given to schemes in which 'pump-priming' is likely to attract sponsorship or charitable donations. Grants will not be provided for schemes which are not of clear museological benefit; nor will they be given for customer service provision such as toilets, sales facilities, cloakrooms and lecture rooms. This might seem rather tough on the museum customer who will normally only be aware of the 'front of house' activities and facilities. However, with a limited budget at its disposal, it is sensible for an AMC to adopt these priorities bearing in mind that there are other Government funded agencies (eg. Tourist Boards) which can provide grant-aid towards visitor facilities such as toilets and car parks.

Effective liaison with other funding agencies is vital if resources available to museums are to be maximised. It is encouraging for example, that Area Councils are beginning to make reciprocal arrangements with Tourist Boards so that senior staff can attend each others management committee meetings. More regular contact with regional offices of the Manpower Services Commission, with Local Education Authorities and with Regional Arts Associations in England and Wales are highly desirable. The London Museums Service (part of the Area Museum Service for South Eastern England) has recently published funding guidelines for independent museums in London. Directed at the London Boroughs Grants Scheme and at other potential funding bodies its objectives are stated as follows:

a) to ensure that funding decisions are made in the most effective and informed way;
b) to aid the distribution of funds against professionally-assessed criteria;
c) to enable major funding bodies in London to adopt a co-ordinated approach to established museums and new museum projects.

Bearing in mind that there are now well over 200 museums in Greater London and a new project seems to spring up virtually every month the need for such guidelines is clear.

So far I have discussed the eligibility principles and general priorities laid down by Area Museum Councils and the need to maximise resources through close liaison with other funding agencies. But what about the individual work programmes of museums – should they also be assessed before grant-aid is provided? The answer is almost certainly 'yes', but there is a delicate balance to be struck between an 'arms-length' assessment of a work programme and interference in the way a museum should be run. The first recommendation that appears in the *Review of Area Museum Councils and Services* states that – 'AMC Directors and their staff should not attempt, either directly or indirectly, to dictate to local museums directors and curators how they should run their museums'. Or put another way, it should never be forgotten that Area Councils were established as the servants of museums and not *vice versa*. The relationship between the Area Council Director and individual curators is obviously vital, and while much depends on personalities, the training and experience of these key members of staff is also an important consideration. Sensitive AMC officers take into account the training and experience of local museum staff with whom they are dealing.

The representative nature of the Area Council's Board of Management also needs to be in balance if the Director of an AMC is to be given the confidence he/she needs when implementing approved policies. The *Review of Area Museum Councils and Services* made a number of recommendations concerning the composition of an AMC's Board of Management – in particular it recommended that at least one half of the members should be museum professionals or other experts. It also argues for a better balance between the number of members from the Local Authority Sector and other types of museums eg. University, Independent and

Armed Forces Museums. In general, this balance is beginning to be achieved.

The Scottish Museums Council is almost certainly the most advanced of the Area Museum Councils in terms of adopting a policy which encourages consideration of a museum's grant-aid application in the context of a defined work programme. The difficulties likely to be experienced by small independent museums without professional curators has prevented the submission of a 3-5 year development plan becoming a condition of grant-aid for 1988/89. However, over the past five years the Scottish Museums Council has actively encouraged museums to develop these mid-term plans which have been formally approved by their Councils or Trustees. The key areas in which planning is recommended to take place are care of collections and collections management, interpretation, research, marketing and financial planning. One of the objectives is to ensure that the Council is not supporting one-off schemes which fall outwith the context of an agreed development plan. The days when curators requested grant-aid towards a variety of equipment (without thinking precisely how it was to be used) simply because it was an easy way to demonstrate to their management committee that they were doing a good job by raising outside money, are numbered.

Although Area Councils are best known for the conservation, technical and design services they provide (directly or indirectly) at subsidised rates, and for the travelling exhibitions they circulate, the trend is currently towards a shift of resources in favour of what can be broadly labelled 'advisory services'. This is a trend which is also evident amongst English Regional Arts Associations which are the counterparts of English Area Museum Councils in the fields of contemporary visual and performing arts. Because the Area Museums Service for South Eastern England covers a large and complex geographical area with a bigger concentration of museums than any other area in the UK, it has almost inevitably taken the lead in its provison of advisory services. The *Review of Area Museum Councils and Services* recommended that each member museum should receive at least one free visit a year from an AMC's senior member of staff. Until recently this seemed an impossible dream in the South-East but AMSSEE has now appointed no fewer than four regional development officers – one for London, and one each for the east, west and south divisions of its area. These development officers advise museums in their divisions on a host of general matters but each officer is also expected to specialise in a subject such as marketing and sponsorship. This specialist expertise is then made available by arrangement throughout the whole AMSSEE area.

AMSSEE has also recognised the need for specialist curatorial advice in certain neglected areas – both geographically and subject-wise. For example, pump-priming funds have been provided for the establishment of what can almost be termed peripatetic curators in Cambridgeshire and Suffolk. These counties are predominantly rural areas with a relatively large number of small, mainly independent museums without professional staff. AMSSEE has also recognised the general lack of curatorial and conservation advice concerning geological collections by appointing a peripatetic geological curator. Originally funded by a MGC Conservation grant this post is now sponsored by British Gas.

The provision of conservation advice has always been a tricky problem for hard-pressed Area Museum Council conservators who have to meet pre-determined income targets. The Scottish Museums Council has led the way by appointing a professional conservator to the post of full-time conservation advisor. Amongst many benefits, the appointment of such a person means that a more aggressive policy of preventative conservation can be pursued. It is quite likely that other AMCs will follow the SMC's example by making similar appointments.

Another development has been the new emphasis on training programmes for museum staff. The Scottish Museums Council and AMSSEE have both appointed training officers and most Area Museum Councils now run a wide range of training courses and seminars. Some of these seminars are linked to formal training programmes such as the Museums Association's Diploma, but many are 'free-standing' and deal with everything from the management of museums to the technical aspects of transporting exhibitions. The MGC's recently published report on *Museum Professional Training and Career Structure* comes out strongly in favour of AMCs developing their training role and recommends the creation of a comprehensive network of regional training officers who would assist the co-ordination of training under the 'umbrella' of a proposed independent national training council.

It is surprising how many museum staff can feel isolated even in cities like London. Visits by AMC development officers and specialist staff and the opportunity to attend locally organised training courses can make all the difference to morale as well as up-dating or teaching new skills. The provision of newsletters and information sheets also provides a vital communication link between AMCs and their members. Every AMC now provides a regular newsletter (sometimes in conjunction with a Regional Museums Federation) and the standard of these publications has risen enormously in the last few years.

The quality of AMC staff and museum staff, particularly the director or curator, is of critical importance if the AMC is to do its work effectively. A good relationship must exist between the Director of the Area Museum Council and museums' governing bodies. AMC directors are increasingly being asked to advise on job descriptions and salary scales for senior museum posts and they are also invited to serve on interview panels. In this way AMCs can improve the likelihood of a fruitful relationship with the museum's future development.

Finally, no review of AMC training and advisory work would be complete without mention of the ubiquitous feasibility study in respect of new museum developments. Everyone knows that museums are a growth industry and a growth industry always attracts consultants. Whether or not the Area Museum Council is directly concerned with recommending and/or grant-aiding a consultant to undertake a feasibility study it is almost inevitable that the consultant will turn to the AMC for advice and information at some stage. The proper assessment of a new museum's desirability and viability is a vital part of an AMCs work if public funds are to be utilised for long-term benefits.

Assessment of AMCs

The *Review of Area Museum Councils and Services* made a number of recommendations which relate to the assessment of AMCs and their activities. First, the report recommended that Area Councils should regularly review museum provision in their regions and the needs of their museum clients. To assist in implementing this type of review, the report recommended that Review Panels should be set up by AMCs to do the following things:
i)   to review the performance of the AMC by examining expenditure on projects and work undertaken;
ii) to consider future priorities for the whole region;
iii) to consider recommendations for growth and development and changes in AMC policy.

It was envisaged that the Review Panels would report directly to, and work closely with, the AMCs Board of Management and would include a number of members of the Board. It was also proposed that between a half and two thirds of its members should be present or past museum professionals.

Most Area Councils have now established Review Panels but the resulting reports have been somewhat disappointing in terms of an objective assessment. Many

Area Council Directors feel that the role of the Review Panel overlaps too much with that of the Board of Management. This is probably fair comment and it is therefore essential that the Commission should assume an increasingly active role in regularly assessing the work and effectiveness of Area Councils, including those in Scotland and Wales. Our task will be made easier from 1988/89 when all of the English AMCs will have adopted three year corporate plans.

So what are the sort of questions which Area Councils and the Commission should be asking to help ensure that Area Councils provide a high quality cost-effective service to their members? The following questions are merely some examples.

1) Is the balance between direct services and grant-aid to members about right?

I have already referred to a general shift of resources in favour of advisory services. Some Area Councils are going to require more advisory staff than others, depending on the nature, number and distribution of museums in their areas. However, these staff will be appointed, to some extent, at the expense of grant-aid to members. Bearing in mind that these staff costs will probably rise faster than increases in government funding (due to salary awards and increments) it is important that Area Councils project their estimates forward so that their members fully appreciate the implications.

2) If Area Councils directly employ conservators, or designers or display technicians, could their respective jobs be done more cost-effectively, but to the same standard, on an agency basis (ie. by staff employed in museums) or by private contractors?

There is no simple or easy answer to this question. The North West Area Museum Council, for example, directly employs a very large number of conservators because historically there have been few private conservators situated in the area and agency arrangements have proved unsatisfactory. However, the situation needs to be kept under review. At the very least (as the MGC Review of AMCs recommended) conservation and design and display services should compete on an equal footing with the private sector. In this regard the issue of satisfactory standards is an important one. In the field of conservation, many readers will be aware that a Conservation Unit has been established recently by the Museums and Galleries Commission and one of its first

Dancers from the 'Steps Out' Dance Workshop in Glasgow examining crystals before dance interpretation. Part of a Leisure Learning Programme, based on a touring exhibition 'Crystals in Industry' organized at the Hunterian Museum, University of Glasgow, with help from the Scottish Museums Council.

tasks will be to establish a register of approved private conservators (they are also supporting the UKICs initiative to introduce accreditation for conservators). In Scotland the Scottish Development Agency's Conservation Bureau publishes a Directory of private conservators, although I understand that they are not individually approved in the way our Conservation Unit proposes.

3) If Area Councils directly provide touring exhibitions, could this provision be more cost-effectively undertaken by museums themselves if they were provided with grant-aid? In general terms, can the generally high subsidy for touring exhibitions be justified?

Once again, there are no easy answers to these questions. Area Councils such as the Area Museum Service for South Eastern England, and the Yorkshire and Humberside AMC have tried to stimulate touring exhibitions by offering grant-aid to their members, but with no great success. There seem to be a number of reasons for this, including lack of museum staff time and appropriate facilities. Business sponsorship can help to get touring exhibitions off the ground, as the Scottish Museums Council has demonstrated. But at the end of the day is it unreasonable for AMC members to pay more realistic hire charges for these exhibitions?

The MGC's report on Travelling Exhibitions (the Hodgkinson Report) and more recently the Commission's report on Museums in Scotland (the Miles Report), have both made recommendations about meeting the demand for touring exhibitions. So far, additional government resources have been hard to come by. The Commission has been allocated £50,000 in 1988/89 and £75,000 in each of the two succeeding years to establish a small Travelling Exhibitions Unit which will concentrate on acting as an exhibition information exchange. It may also be possible to operate a small grants fund and we will be talking to

Area Councils as to how this money might best be spent.

4) Could Area Councils do more to stimulate collaborative projects between museums (by adjusting their grant-aid priorities) in order to maximise the use of grant-aid?

The next paper describes the benefits of Countywide Consultative Committees and the ways in which they benefit from grant-aid for collaborative projects. However, perhaps I may suggest two areas of co-operation which could be encouraged by offers of grant-aid. First, I believe that museums should be encouraged to develop joint storage schemes, particularly in respect of bulk archaeological material. Through the Commission's capital grants scheme we will do all we can to collaborate with English Area Councils to make progress in this area.

Secondly, I believe that Area Museum Councils should be doing much more to encourage museums to market themselves effectively – and given that most museums have ridiculously small marketing budgets at their disposal, the stimulation of joint marketing schemes is essential. Once again the Commission will do all in its power to help Area Museum Councils. In this connection the Office of Arts and Libraries are providing the Commission with £70,000 in 1988/89, and £100,000 in each of the two succeeding years for 'marketing and management initiatives'. We will obviously be discussing with Area Museum Councils (including the Scottish Museums Council) how this money can best be spent.

Conclusion

In conclusion I can only confirm the Commission's faith in the Area Museum Councils by telling you that Area Councils were once again our top priority when bidding for government resources for the next financial year. We did not get all we wanted but we will be able to pass on approximately 4% increases for all English AMCs, plus some extra money to take into account special factors, (eg. new accommodation).

However, there is no room for complacency. There are still some who advocate that we could do without Area Councils, passing the available government money directly to larger local authority museums who would exercise pastoral care amongst smaller museums in their area. Area Museum Councils will need to take advantage of a variety of income-generating opportunities and demonstrate 'value for money' if they are to maintain their current position in the museum world.

Some co-operative approaches to marketing museums.

Museum Consultative Committees

Crispin Paine

Crispin Paine has been Director of the Area Museums Service for South Eastern England since 1979. Prior to that he was managing museums in Worcester, Stevenage, Oxford City and Oxfordshire.

Introduction

Why is it we talk about the museums 'movement'? For many of us who work in museums, or who work with museums as Friends, volunteers or trustees, it is almost a religious or political cause.

I think I remember the moment of my own conversion. I was at school near Brighton on the south coast of England, where the rolling chalk downs come close to the sea. Now, thanks to nitrates and EEC subsidies, they grow wheat, but formerly they were good for nothing but sheep. The local village had a museum; I'm convinced I can remember one exhibit: a 'life-preserver' or cosh which, the label explained, its shepherd-owner had needed when he walked over the empty grassy hills.

I have never forgotten that history lesson nor how clearly artefacts can speak if properly interpreted. If you laugh at my earnestness I shall blush, but I expect everyone in our profession has some such story to tell.

This fanaticism has created the modern museum service in Britain. A service that is enormously rich in collections, in variety and in the quality of what if offers to the public. But a service that is chaotic, wildly uneven and uncoordinated, and for that reason quite absurdly wasteful of every sort of resource.

Countywide Museums Committees – Aims

I should like to describe the contribution that Countywide Museum Consultative Committees can make to getting us better museums.

A Countywide Museums Committee – I prefer that term because they are by no means merely consultative – is a committee which includes representatives of all the organisations which run museums in a particular county. It includes councillors from County and District Councils, representatives of University museums and trustees from independent museums. It is supported, encouraged and bullied by a County Curators Group which includes the curators of all the county's museums and which is very often the tail that wags the dog.

The Committees' money – sometimes thousands, sometimes scarcely hundreds – comes normally from County and/or District Councils, supplemented by Area Service and other grants, sponsorship and so on.

I imagine I have been asked to write about Countywide Museum Committees because we've got more of them in our Area than anywhere else. That of course is because the South Eastern England Area is quite absurdly big – 20 million people in Greater London and the fifteen surrounding counties, 900 museums. The Area Museums Service for South Eastern England (AMSSEE) has had a deliberate policy, instead of splitting up the Area, of fostering museum cooperation on a countywide basis. We are moving cautiously towards a federal structure with AMSSEE as the Feds and counties as the States.

The first job of a Countywide Museums Committee is to be a talking shop. It is wonderful to see how, given a modicum of goodwill and a strong chairman, a collection of highly suspicious councillors, trustees and University people begin to really work together for the good of museums as a whole. You can always tell when these committees are beginning to gel: it's when instead of sniping at each other they begin to criticise the Area Museums Service and the Museums and Galleries Commission.

The job of the Countywide Committee is to represent the interests of museums in their counties. Their political role is absolutely crucial. They are in a unique position to be able to influence local authorities, to give County Councils for example confidence that the museum community is able to speak with one voice, to ensure that District Councils' leisure and arts development plans take proper notice of museums and mesh with those of neighbouring authorities.

Countywide Museums Committees can also support the Area Museums Service in ensuring that the various quangos use their grants effectively to promote museum development. A splendid recent step forward in London was the London Museums Consultative Committee persuading the Tourist Board, Regional Arts Association and London Boroughs Grants Scheme to accept its funding guidelines.

Museums in Britain are chaotic. The Scottish Museums Council, I think, has showed the way in producing a Development Strategy, its *Framework for Museums in Scotland*, to try to guide the growth of museums. We in AMSSEE are trying to follow this example, but we are turning first to the Countywide Committees to ask them to produce Development Plans for their counties. Three of them are just beginning to tackle the job, and it will of course be the first great test of their effectiveness.

Countywide Museums Committees – Work Programmes

Just as Area Museums Services have a tension between their strategic role and their services to their members, so do Countywide Committees. That's enough of the strategic stuff – what can these animals actually *do* for museums?

The enormous expansion in museum numbers in the UK over the past few years has been very largely due to all the new little local history museums – the community museums. The people who set up and run them bring enormous strengths of enthusiasm, local knowledge, often special skills and links with the community. Very often, though, they do need professional advice and guidance in the straight curatorial field, and this 'pastoral care' to small museums is something many Countywide Museums Committees see as one of their chief roles.

The three county museums officers in my own Area spend a good deal of their time advising and helping voluntary museums, and at the regular meetings of Countywide Museums Committees the voluntary curators come as equal partners.

Because they are so much closer to the grassroots, Countywide Museums Committees are much better placed than Area Museums Services to support and draw-on the smallest of our museums.

Here I want to pause for a tiny history lesson. Local government reorganisation in England took place in 1974, and professional opinion then strongly favoured giving museum powers to counties rather than Districts. In fact they got concurrent powers, and there then started in the more enlightened parts of the country a campaign to persuade Districts and County Councils to pool their resources and put all local government museums under joint management. Where this happened it was an enormous success – some readers may have visited the impressive headquarters of the Hampshire County Museums Service in Winchester during the Museums Association Conference in 1987. Sadly, though, local jealousies or simply lack of money left local government museums in most of England as weak and divided as before.

Can the Countywide Museums Committees find new ways of helping their members pool resources? I believe they can, and the key is going to be shared staff.

Museum people are extremely good at ignoring reality, and for years we have behaved as if some day we will attain a Nirvana where every museum has a full complement of specialist staff to look after its collections. I'm afraid we won't. Meanwhile, though, in hundreds of museums throughout the country there are collections of major scientific importance lying neglected and uncurated for want of anyone who knows anything about them. Survey after survey shows this to be true in geology, ethnography, natural history, military history, the fine and decorative arts, and so on.

We have got, at the tail end of the 20th century, to grasp this nettle. We must do two things: we must relocate collections from museums where they are unloved to museums where they can be given specialist care. If you haven't got a geologist on your staff, what on earth are you doing with rocks and fossils in your stores? Place them on permanent loan with a museum with a geologist. And we have got to begin sharing staff

between museums: instead of two neighbouring museums with archaeological curators but no social historian, we will have an archaeologist and a social historian shared between the two.

Here, of course, we are treading on local sensibilities and tripping over problems of salary differentials, employment policies and so on and on. Countywide Museums Committees, I suggest, are best placed to improve the cost-effectiveness of curatorial provision. They already bring together the authorities which run the museums and I look forward to them appointing peripatetic curators, planning relocation of specialist collections and planning a rational pattern of qualified curators to look after them.

Countywide Museums Committees can help their member museums directly with conservation and the care of their collections. One Committee in the AMSSEE Area has commissioned a survey of the conservation needs of its museums, while another is hoping to secure County Council support for the setting up of a conservation laboratory which will do conservation work for all museums in the county.

I hope that over the next few years in the South East we shall see the setting up of conservation laboratories dealing with general antiquities in many, if not all, the counties in the Area. AMSSEE will then be left with the job of providing specialised conservation at an Area level – in paintings, natural science, textiles, engineering and so on.

I expect too that we shall see Countywide Museums Committees setting up joint stores for their members. The first ones will probably be archaeological stores, but these will be followed by stores for large items like agricultural machinery and later for general antiquities. Such stores will be built to a high standard providing proper security and environmental control, will be professionally curated and will usually have a conservation facility attached. It may sound expensive, but it will be much better value than the present pattern of inadequate and highly expensive town centre stores.

These are the days of marketing initiatives, tourism, the role of visitor attractions in economic regeneration, and we are all worrying about the role of museums in the booming leisure industry or about the package of public services our museums can offer. I wonder if we aren't in danger of forgetting the real nature of museums, of enjoying the sweet fruit but throwing away the kernel? After all, what is a museum? Basically it is a great and unique body of *information*, information which resides in the objects and their accompanying documentation, both together. It is on this body of information that a museum bases the services it offers to the public: without it a museum becomes a mere theme park or heritage centre or funfair.

So many parts of the museum world seem to be forgetting this fundamental point. The recent Hale Report spent pages worrying about the training of managers, conservators, security men in museums, but scarcely mentioned the central role of the curator in caring for the body of information in a scholarly sense.

What I am talking about, then, is scholarship. Its become almost a dirty word in some quarters – but isn't it time we rediscovered scholarship as the core of the curator's job: to build up the museum's collections and information as a unique information bank?

I should like to suggest that this is another area in which local groups of museums, perhaps Countywide Museums Committees, could do something really useful.

Social history museums, in particular, need help. What we need is for all the social history museums in a county to come together and agree on a research programme which divides up the work according to each museum's

ability. It implies an agreed publications programme, shared *academic* training, and a common research and collecting programme.

At present too many social history museums collect randomly without any real concept of what information they are seeking, without any real scholarly purpose. We aren't, bluntly, going to get a Swedish-style national research policy in this country, so why not start locally? A Countywide Museums Committee which has already learned to work together is, I suggest, the best body to get a modest initiative going.

I have been talking about museum cooperation within counties, but remember there's nothing magic about the county itself – it's simply that for an awful lot of joint schemes a local group of twenty, thirty or forty museums of different shapes and sizes is about right. Again, those readers who were at the 1987 Museums Association Conference, may have seen something of the Defence of the Realm Heritage project. This is a marketing campaign to promote the army, navy and airforce museums of the Portsmouth area – about fifty of them, from the Mary Rose to a medieval castle. The campaign has a full-time staff and has been hugely successful, well justifying the local authorities' and Tourist Boards' investment.

A county would be an excellent basis for a similar marketing campaign, though so far I know of only one Countywide Museums Committee which has ventured more than the usual publicity leaflet, posters and stand at the County Fair. Cambridgeshire is shortly to launch a campaign to promote the museums of Cambridge, and that I'm sure will be a campaign properly based on a market analysis. I look forward to seeing many other Committees taking on this role.

The flavour of the month just at the moment is of course training. There is no doubt that many (most?) of us in museums are abominably badly trained. Even if museums are immeasurably more complex organisations than the small businesses, theatres or sports centres with which they are often compared, there's no excuse for the way in which we constantly have to reinvent the wheel (more or less round) simply for want of training.

Things are about to get very much better. The Museums Association is going to replace its Diploma with a range of distance-learning packages covering the whole spectrum of jobs done in museums. The Museums and Galleries Commission's Hale Report has proposed a way of giving museum training a real kick forwards.

But if you are a businessman on the Trust of an open-air museum, a housewife on the committee of a local history museum or a factory worker working as a volunteer in a nature reserve, you want your training to be very local indeed.

A number of Countywide Museums Committees are running training seminars at different venues around their counties. I spoke recently at one on fund-raising where the audience included enthusiasts from a model railway museum, curators from University museums, and trustees of two community museums.

If this pattern could be spread throughout the country and be backed up with distance-learning packages we would see a dramatic rise in the standards of our local museums.

One of the fields in which Countywide Museums Committees have had particular success is documentation – the cataloguing of museum collections. One has had a team from the Manpower Services Commission working for the past five years cataloguing the collections of the county's small museums: the next step is to computerise so as to produce a Union Catalogue of all the museum objects in the county. In another county an MSC team is

photographing the collections. A third Committee published a thesaurus of terms which is now in use in many museums throughout Britain.

I could go on listing the areas where an active Countywide Museums Committee could help guide and support its museums. They could be doing more to present the cause of museums to councillors, MPs and so on. They could (and some of them do) make use of their links with the Local Education Authority to promote the cause of museum education.

I will mention one last activity of Countywide Museums Committees, and one which I'm less enthusiastic about. Some of them give small grants to their smaller museums. How useful are grants? We suffer from a barrage of propaganda at present about 'challenge' grants and 'incentive funding', but just how effective are they? I suspect that big museums don't get challenged because they don't really need the money – it's just a useful extra; small museums can't afford to meet the challenge, and medium-sized museums, while they certainly welcome and use grants, are themselves initiating the schemes rather than really responding to outside 'incentive' or 'challenge'. However, I confess I have yet to meet anyone who shares this cynical view.

So how does one develop a Countywide Museums Committee? Well, first form a County Curators' Group and have them work together long enough to trust one another and have a common view on life. Then you need three things: first, a senior officer in a major local authority who will sell the idea to the local authorities at a senior level; second, a councillor of some weight who will give the Committee their commitment and enthusiasm, and third, you need a representative of the independent museums who can persuade them to join in. Find these things and you can get the benefits I believe a Countywide Museums Committee can bring. You may even find you have a stick to beat your Area Museums Service with!

Developing the quality of customer service – lessons for museums from the High Street.

Museums in the United Kingdom – the development of a profession

Graeme Farnell

Graeme Farnell, a former Director of the Scottish
Museums Council, is now Director General of the
Museums Association.

Introduction

Development implies looking forwards. In this paper I
shall look at how we might develop an enhanced
professionalism in the future. To do that, I think we
need to ask two questions. First: what are the key issues
the museum profession faces at the present time? And
second what aims might we set ourselves over the next
five years or so?

Let me say right at the outset that I see my contribution
very much as continuing a discussion, developing a
dialogue with professional colleagues, and perhaps
provoking debate. Certainly not handing down tablets
of stone.

So, first of all, what are the key issues which we now
face as a profession?

First of all I'd like to say what I think those issues are
not.

I don't think it's a question of low salaries, outrageously
inadequate though many of them are.

I don't think it's about our ever-reducing budgets.

I don't think it's about privatisation, although this is
obviously an ever-increasing possibility for those of us
in the local authority sector.

I don't think it's about the conglomerate leisure
departments which are springing up all over the
country with far-reaching – and generally bad –
consequences for museums and their staff.

And I don't even think that one of our key issues is the
selling of museum collections, even though this is a
trend which is increasing – and which, some might
argue, is being given covert government support.

I'm not saying that all these things aren't important.
They are certainly very much on people's minds. They
are also things on which the Museums Association is
taking, and will continue to take, action because they
are all issues which certainly affect the museum
community – normally in an adverse way.

Let me give just three examples of the Association's

action: right at the moment we are fighting to avoid a leading major museums service being subsumed in a faceless Leisure Department – and we shall issue definitive guidance to authorities on this issue. We are fighting the government's proposed Miscellaneous Provisions Bill giving some of our national institutions powers of sale which none – save the government – want. And I am especially delighted that the Association is on the verge of commissioning an independent, authoritative salary survey in the New Year, with financial support from the Museums and Galleries Commission.

But, nevertheless, I don't think that these are the really key issues which are facing us at the moment.

Why do I say this? Well, because they're all responding to threats from outside the museum community. On none of them are museums themselves taking the initiative, on all of them we are forced to be reactive rather than proactive. Ultimately, even if we were to win on all those issues, would that necessarily improve the quality of our museums for the people that are using them?

All the issues I've mentioned, however important they are, are basically inward-looking. And arguably they are also issues about which our users, our customers if you like, really don't care that much. In other words, they may be problems for us but they're not problems for the vast majority of people that use us. No, I'd like to suggest that the key issues facing the profession are in fact managerial ones. As we all know, there's been declining growth in public sector funding in the UK over the last decade. What we've seen during that time is a steady shift of emphasis away from growth in services and towards actively managing change. In other words, the challenge now is to get the same – or more – from less resources. And essentially this boils down to a change from administration and towards management.

So, I would argue that the key issues for the profession are managerial ones. And I think there are three of them. First of all, what business are we really in? Second, how can we improve customer service? And third, do we have the right attitude to change? I think on all these three issues we in the museum profession can actually take the initiative. The onus is on us to start things happening, and we're not being forced under duress to respond to some crisis which is being provoked from the outside.

More importantly, none of these issues – none of the actions we have to take on them – is going to cost us a fortune. In fact, very much of what we have to do about them won't cost us a penny. Even more important, we don't need more staff in order to do anything about them either. And it seems to me that if we do take action on some of these issues it'll have a massive impact on the quality of our museums as far as our users are concerned. So basically, I would argue that since it's not going to cost us cash, since we don't need lots more staff, and since the result of action in these areas *is* going to be significant improvement in the quality of our museums, in fact as a profession we've got no excuses left *not* to take the action that's required.

What business are we in?

So turning the first of these issues – what business are we in? I think there's an interesting challenge for each of us to sum up – in no more than a maximum of two or three words – what business our own museum is actually in.

Let's look at a few analogies. In the cosmetics industry basically what they identify as their business is not selling cosmetics at all but the business of 'beauty'. Or, to take another analogy, the insurance business, or the security, or the fire fighting business – all these businesses are actually in the business of selling not their products but 'peace of mind'. Or to take another analogy, the Church is no longer really in the business of religion. It's really nowadays in the business of providing 'companionship'. And the essence of all these parallels is that the companies involved have identified how their particular business *benefits* their customers. In other words, each of them is offering some *promise* to the customer.

There's a whole host of different answers possible to the question 'what business are we in?' Some museums may be in the leisure learning business, others are perhaps in the communication business, still others may be in the research business, while others, particularly perhaps in Scotland, are essentially in the business of community development or even economic development. What I'd like to emphasise is that I don't think there's any *right* answer to the question. The fact that there is a diverse range of answers possible, simply means that our museums are that much richer and that they offer an appetising variety of experiences for their users.

But what I think *is* vital, is that each museum director is absolutely clear about his or her own museum's role – about his or her own museum's particular business. Asking the question 'what business are we in?' on the one hand helps us to define, to hone down our area of activitiy. At the same time, it opens up new possibilities of action for each of us. It's an essential first step. The worrying fact is that very many – perhaps even most – museums have very little idea what business they *are* actually in. To simply ask that question, to think about that question, is in itself the first step towards success.

When we know what business we're in we can start to ask, 'Why are we here?' 'What's our museum's purpose?' 'What are we being paid to do?' In other words, we can formulate what in the USA tends to be called a 'mission statement'.

I'd like to give a couple of examples of mission statements from the business world and a couple of examples from the museum field.

The first example I'd like to look at is Avis Rent-a-Car. A few years back Avis was in trouble, its business was going down and it certainly wasn't thriving. What the company decided to do was to spend three months or so just concentrating on looking at what business they were in. At that time they were involved in a whole range of different activities, hotels, restaurants – all sorts of things apart from just the car hire business. As a result of this three-month introspecion they were able to sum up their business in just three words – 'renting driverless vehicles'. Then what they did was to sell off their interest in hotels, restaurants and so on and simply concentrate on that main line of business. And as a result the business began to flourish.

A few months ago in some of our daily papers there were full page ads taken out by a company that wanted to explain its new mission statement to the public. That company was TI, Tube Investments, the people who make – or used to make – Creda cookers, Raleigh bikes and so on. TI has also been ailing in recent years and needed to redefine its mission in order to succeed. The new statement they came up with was: 'to become an international engineering group concentrating on specialised engineering businesses, operating in selected niches on a global basis.' And as a result what they're gradually doing is moving out of the fast moving consumer goods field (such as Raleigh cycles which they have now sold off) and they're buying up – going into – far more specialised fields.

Many years ago when I was a student at university and when it was quite easy to get a job during the summer vacation, I used to work in Burtons. In those days it called itself 'The Tailor of Taste'. Well, those days have changed. And Burtons has of course moved out of the field of simply tailoring and into what they now call the business of 'speciality retailing'. As a result, over the last decade turnover has increased from £7 million to over £150 million a year.

So a mission statement, a new definition of purpose, can

lead to a number of different things. It can lead to retrenchment, in the case of Avis Rent-a-Car. To re-structuring, in the case of TI. Or − and this will appeal to the empire builders among us − to massive expansion in the case of Burtons!

But what about the museums field, what sort of examples can we look at of organisations that have developed a clear mission statement?

Well the first is the Scottish Museums Council itself which is in the business of 'improving the quality of local museum and gallery provision in Scotland'.

The Museums Association itself has been looking at this problem over the last few months and I'd like to look in a little more detail at the process which we've gone through and at what the result has been.

The first thing we had to do was to try to identify what was the promise, what was the benefit, that we were offering to our 3,000 members. Now quite a lot of these, particularly the individuals, are paying quite a lot of money each year for a range of benefits which are not that immediately obvious: publications; attending conferences and seminars; receiving advice and support and so on. But essentially it didn't seem to us that people were paying that sort of money just for those relatively few tangible benefits. This is very often the case. The benefits which we *think* our organisation or museum is offering are actually not the benefits which our customers really find important. And very often, our customers (our users) find that what's most important to them is actually something quite abstract, quite intangible. And this, I think, is the case with the Association.

One of our national museums recently commissioned a MORI survey which illustrates the way in which the public's perceptions can differ from those of the profession. It looked at nine different museum functions, each of which were rated as more or less important by, in turn, the general public, museum directors, attendant staff, MP's and industrialists. The differences were striking. 'Identifying objects' scored 69% on the relative importance scale from directors, but only 21% from the public. 'Displaying historical objects' scored 59% from directors, but only 34% from the public.

Incidentally, the survey also asked about attitudes to both local and national museums, with the − rather chilling − attitudinal response from the public, only 27% of whom felt that 'local museums do a better job of making themselves more attractive than the major national museums'. This poor perception was emphasised even more strongly by industrialists, only 13% of whom felt local museums did a better job.

But let's come back to the Association. What we identified as the benefit we were offering our members was essentially *status*. Now those members that are here will immediately tell me whether we're right or wrong in identifying that as the main benefit. But certainly the people we've spoken to so far have agreed that *yes* − the thing that they're really wanting from the Association is status. Status in a context in which museums are often at the bottom of local government priorities, for example, and in which museums are perceived quite often rather negatively by the media and sections of the public. What people working in museums are looking for is an endorsement of their worth to their peers and to society as a whole. It's that need which essentially their membership of the Association was meeting − and particularly was endorsing through the Associateship and Fellowship of the Association.

So when we'd identified the benefits of the Association, or if you like what business we were in, the business of conferring status, we were then able to look at what our mission, what our purpose in life is. And eventually, after lots of discussion internally and informal discussions with lots of our members, we've come up with a mission statement which has been approved by our Council. We see our role as being to 'enhance the professionalism and the standing of the museum community'.

In that statement there are three key words. The first is 'professionalism' which is something that people who work in museums care passionately about and talk very frequently and very proudly about. The second important word is 'standing' – in other words status – which is another thing which, as I've said, is of great importance to everybody involved with museums. And the third important word is 'community', the 'museum community'. By that phrase, we want to embrace not only these staff that work in museums but also all those people who help out in a voluntary capacity and – most important – all those people who serve on committees, or boards of museums, and to indicate in the term 'community' that all these people have – or should have – a commonality of interest, should all be pulling in the same direction and should all have the same concerns at heart. That concern should be to strive for excellence in our museums, for the very best service to the people who use our museums. This feeling of unity between people who happen to have different roles in the museum community is a very important issue for the Association. To put an artificial divide between people who happen to be paid to do a job within museums and those who happen to be working on a free basis for museums, or who happen to be working on an advisory basis for museums as a committee or board member is a completely artificial, negative and needless kind of separation. In saying that, I am not saying that there is always necessarily a commonality of view between each of those contituencies. What I am saying is that it is in everybody's interest, and particularly in museum users' interests, that there should be a creative dialogue and that there should be a striving towards a commonality of purpose between each of these players on the museum scene.

But some of you may well be saying, well all this is a waste of time. If you ask the question what business are museums in, there's a very simple answer. That is museums are in the museum business. If you ask what their purpose its, what their mission is, then there's also a very simple answer and that is that museums collect, document, preserve, exhibit and interpret – that's their purpose and their role. Now I have to admit that those two answers have some merit. They're very simple. They're very straightforward.

But, the problem with those two answers is that actually they don't get us anywhere. Because if we're simply saying that museums are in the museum business and are there to do all the things that museums do, the trouble is that in terms of direction for your museum and in terms of setting priorities for it in the context of a shrinking budget, it actually doesn't help at all.

And I think there's another problem. It's a very introverted view. Because, after all, museums don't exist for museum staff. They actually exist for the community – for the people out there that are going to be using us – and surely the purpose of a museum, its mission, must actually identify fundamentally the museum's *value* to its community. So the problem with the 'museum is a museum,' standpoint is that it's not people-centered at all. It's not user-centered. It's introspective and introverted. And it's not going to get us anywhere.

But, you might well ask, how is any sort of definition of purpose going to be directly helpful to *me* in my everyday work – given all the incredible pressures which I and my staff are subject to – we just don't have time to bother with this sort of thing.

Well, I do think that a definition of purpose is worthwhile spending some time on. First of all, if you've got a clear purpose things are going to change. Having a mission is a springboard towards planning – planning for the future – which I know is something that the

Scottish Museums Council is very keen to encourage. And I think it's the essential first step in that planning process.

Secondly, it's an excellent way of communicating. The dialogue which you have to have about your mission involves your staff, involves your committee members or trustees and involves members of your community in thinking about what the museum is there to achieve. That very process in itself is helpful in building unity of purpose, in building internal strength within the museum.

But having a mission also helps with prioritising the museum's programmes. It seems to me that what we should be working towards is not a situation in which the same old programmes, the same old things roll on year after year simply because they've always been done. But a situation in which we're very clear about our mission, about what we're wanting to achieve, about what our specific objectives and tasks are. We are then creative about thinking about what sort of programmes – what sort of activities – we need to develop in order to reach those objectives. It may well be that our programmes, our activities, change from year to year in order to meet the objectives that your museum has set for itself. That makes, I think, for a much more exciting environment to work in and a much more interesting museum for the public to come and use.

Having a mission is also critically important to fundraising. If you can be clear about what your museum is wanting to achieve then it's going to be that much easier to excite, motivate, and involve the business community, charitable trusts, and philanthropic individuals in helping your museum to get there. But if you can't be clear about your purpose in the first place you're never going to attract that sort of support, or at least to any considerable extent.

Finally, thinking about and developing and having a mission statement is a marvellous way of stimulating creative thinking about your museum and its activities.

So, the first issue I think we in the museum profession need to face is to identify what business it is we're in. To identify what our mission is. This is one of the essential questions any museum has to ask if it is really going to be successful. The answers to that question should be user-orientated and should result in fundamental and practical improvements to what the museum is actually doing.

How can we improve user service?

So, let's turn to the second key issue I believe the museum profession has to face. What about user service? How can we improve user service?

Whether we like it or not, museums are there to serve their customers – to serve their users. When we think about it, this range of users is incredibly wide. What does it include? Well, it includes the casual visitor, the family group, the person who has dropped in for 10 minutes because he's got nothing else to do. It includes expert research workers, who are in the lead in their highly specialised field. It includes schools – anything from four year olds up to 18 year olds. It may include national minority groups, disabled people. It may include businessmen. It may include tourists. The range of our clients is incredibly varied. It's a very complex mix that we are serving and I think it's also a very difficult mix to serve really well.

If we look at shops it's an interesting analogy. One of the clear trends we've seen in the last five years or so is that shops are now becoming increasingly specialised – they're starting up new chains, new types of shops to appeal to particular market segments, to particular homogeneous sections of the population that are of the same age or have the same interests – have the same

Fun with Fossils. Young visitors exploring prehistoric times at Hamilton District Museum – part of the educational activities associated with the Hunterian Museum's touring exhibition 'Mr. Wood's Fossils'.

values, if you like. Whoever would have thought that a tiny franchise would sell socks, or ties, and would be so enormously successful? Or that a shop called *Objects*, with its merchandise displayed in museum-type show cases, would be a massive hit?

And in the museum field, I think a couple of analogous developments have taken place in the London museums, in the shape of the 'Boiler House' – as was – at the Victoria and Albert Museum and at 'Launch Pad' at the Science Museum. Here you've got, if you like, two museum brands. Two parts of museums – galleries of

museums – which have been quite aggressively promoted by the host museums as having strong individual identities. In other words, people go (or rather went) to the Boiler House simply to see what was on at the Boiler House. They weren't interested in the rest of the V & A. Similarly with 'Launch Pad'. You take your kids along to 'Launch Pad' and that's all you go to see. You don't go to see the rest of the Science Museum. In that way these museums were targeting very specific audiences. The young, designer-conscious in the case of Boiler House and parents with kids in the case of 'Launch Pad'. Both of course have been enormously successful. I think it maybe reflects a new style of thinking about the range of offerings we have in our museums and how we can target those to the various market sectors.

But let's get back to the question of user service. The first thing that's very clear is that this doesn't have a very high profile on the profession's current agenda.

At the Museums Association we run quite a lot of in-service training seminars. The ones that we always find most difficult to fill, in fact the ones which are nearly always threatened with cancellation, are the ones on customer care. There is very little written in the professional journals about how to care for our customers. Surely the everyday experience of all of us is that when we go to visit another museum, the quality of care for us as a member of the visiting public certainly usually leaves something to be desired. There isn't always that welcome, that friendliness, that visible concern for us as members of the public, that surely there should be.

The parallel with shops here is quite uncanny. *The Times* recently carried a report on the results of a national survey carried out by the advertising agency, Leo Burnett. It looked at how customers responded to quality of service in shops. It found that an overwhelming 91% of people were refusing to return to shops where they had experienced bad service and not only are 72% of customers demanding better service – 70% are actually prepared to pay more for it! The most successful shops are now involved in training their 'sales consultants' in such sophisticated skills as body language or how to approach a customer – a quality of training that is a million miles away from what is being taught to most of our attendant staff, who perform – in part at least – a similar kind of interface with the public.

Why is quality of user service an essential issue for the profession?

Well, I think it's quite simply that we can't afford to alienate our customers in an era in which there is ever-increasing competition for those customers. Not only between different museums, but increasingly between the whole range of new leisure attractions (of which shopping is one); and increasingly between museums and the leisure activities taking place in peoples' own homes – video, television, hi-fi, computer games, reading, knitting and so on. And poor customer care is certainly not good for museums' image as a whole. It's certainly not good for the learning experience which we offer our users – if a visitor isn't made to feel welcome and relaxed then he's not going to respond as positively to our exhibitions and he's not going to be as receptive to the messages or experiences that we're offering him. Finally, and really importantly, it's actually not very satisfying for our staff to work in an environment in which customer care isn't given real priority. Nobody likes to work in an organisation which really doesn't care about the people that are its bread and butter. That sort of approach breeds very low morale and poor satisfaction with the job that people are doing.

I'd like to emphasise that in talking about people who come to the museum as customers, or users, I'm not implying that museums are only important as exhibitions, or places for casual visitors to see things. I was, for example, enormously impressed to see at the National Museums on Merseyside two new high quality developments which cater to the needs of specific users. A superb Natural History Centre, equipped with microscopes, computers and laboratory equipment, where visitors – helped by seven staff – can handle, analyse and generally learn more through direct interaction with collections which until that time had languished in storage. And a marvellous ceramics study gallery, equipped with safe handling facilities and computer databases with documentation about the collections. That, too, is user service of a high quality.

So, if we want to improve customer care, where do we

start? Well, I think the first thing we have to do is to know what quality, or level service our users actually want.

Believe it or not the MacDonalds fast food chain can offer us an interesting lesson here. They give customer service a very high priority indeed. How they went about developing that quality of customer service was this – and it was incredibly logical. First, they evaluated what the customer actually wanted from MacDonalds. They went out and they *talked* to their customers – and I want to emphasise that it's not just a question of costly questionnaires that have to be administered by some sort of professional organisation, some consultancy. It's really a question of getting out there and talking to the people that are actually using your facility. This is what MacDonalds did and they found that their customers were concerned about quality, and predictability, about speed of service, about absolute cleanliness and about friendliness of staff. Having found out what it was that the customers thought important about MacDonalds, they then set standards of performance in each of those areas that they had pinpointed. The next thing that they did was that they trained their staff to perform to those standards. Finally what they did – and this is where I think it's more difficult for museums to follow suit – is that they set their levels of pay in relation to the attainment of those standards. In other words, if I don't actually meet the standards of performance for customer service that are laid down by MacDonalds then I don't get as much cash in my pay packet at the end of the week as someone who has. Obviously that's a very powerful motivating factor.

The quality, the standard, of service that our users are looking for may not always be what we think they are looking for. This is why we have to ask them. It may be that we in museums are providing in some areas too high a standard of service in relation to what the customers really want. More likely than not, too low a

standard in other areas which are *really* important to customers.

Starting to improve the quality of our service need not be as complex as we might at first think. There's a very useful concept here that we can look at and that is the concept of having a very small number of *key* contact points between our users and ourselves. Each of these key contact points – and there's probably only 4 or 5 of them – have to be excellently managed. It's the old 80/20 syndrome isn't it? It's actually only 20% of what we're doing that really matters and makes a difference and the 80% of what we're doing we needn't pay as much attention to. So what are some of these key contact points as far as museums are concerned? Those few points we really have to manage well?

Well, as far as the Association is concerned we're getting fairly clear about what they are. First of all, answering the telephone – the very first contact that many of our members have with us. How quickly is the 'phone answered? How friendly and helpful is the person at the other end of the 'phone? Another key contact for us is the time at which you renew your annual subscription – the letter that you get with your subscription renewal, the speed at which your membership card comes to you after you've paid your money. And another key contact point is obviously when you actually come to the Museum Association offices themselves and the environment and the welcome which you get when you come there.

So what are some of the key contact points for our museums? It's almost certainly the initial person-to-person contact that the visitor has with whichever member of staff is nearest the door – usually a member of the attendant or shop staff. It's certainly the first impression that your museum entrance, your signposting, your name gives to the visitor as he finds himself in this new and possibly strange – and possibly even threatening – environment.

So, I would argue that improving the quality of our service to our users is a vital issue for all of us. I think it is essential because our future depends on it, because customer satisfaction depends on it and because staff satisfaction also depends on it. It's actually quite easy for us to improve. All we have to do is to find out what level of quality of service our users actually want and then steadily train our staff, make our staff aware of those standards, and encourage them to provide those standards. But what is absolutely essential is that the person at the top of the museum organisation is fully committed to improving the quality of user service and can demonstrate *personally*, on a daily basis, to all his or her staff that this is a really important task for them to get right.

Do we have the right attitude to change?

A third issue that I think is important for the profession at the moment is the question of whether we have the right attitude to change.

There's no doubt that we're in a time of change. We've got the whole issue of plural funding which is now virtually taken for granted and essentially, of course, this means less public sector funding as a proportion of the whole. We've got much more competition both for cash for our museums, and as I mentioned, for the public's leisure time. We've got a change in our profile of visitors as the age range within our society changes. We've got de-municipilisation of services and we've got, not least, the exponential increase in the number of museums themselves. So there's no doubt that we are in a period of quite rapid change.

But what is our attitude to these changes that are taking place?

During our Conference in Bournemouth this year we ran a couple of what we call focus group interviews, or rather a firm of consultants ran them for us. They got together a group of a dozen or so people chosen at random and talked to them about what the key issues for the profession were. Many of the issues that I've mentioned earlier in this talk were brought up by that random selection of individuals. But the striking thing about the result of the focus group interviews was that overall there was a very, very pessimistic response coming from those people about the whole range of issues affecting the profession. That's worrying because I believe we're over-estimating the threats. We are over-estimating the problems that are confronting the profession. Putting it very crudely, I think it's just too easy to categorise our situation as on the one hand facing a completely uninterested, unsympathetic central government and an increasingly polarised and politicised local government. In other words at no level – goes an often-stated professional view – is there any sort of genuine support or real political or financial commitment to museums.

The first thing to say about change surely is that we shouldn't be surprised about it. In fact, it can actually be the result of success. And it can also actually mean improvement. And it *should* also mean seizing opportunities.

The management writer, Peter Drucker, has said this:

> 'Rapid growth in an industry is one of the most reliable and easily spotted indicators of impending change in that industry's structure. Its structure will change drastically – at the very latest by the time it has doubled in volume.'

So, if we look at museums and the way in which they've increased exponentially in actual numbers, and in numbers of visitors they are attracting, and in their budgets and so on over the last 10 or 20 years, surely that's exactly the situation that we're in. We've got an industry here that has doubled its volume and its structure as a result is going to be changing dramatically. But inherent in those very changes we have massive opportunities. And in order to capitalise on those opportunities museums have fabulous strengths.

First of all we've got in a great many cases superb buildings right in the middle of cities or towns. In other words property, and property locations, that are often the envy of any retailer for example.

The High Street on display – new social history display at the McManus Galleries, Dundee.

Dundee Museums and Art Galleries.

We've got over 73 million visits a year to museums in the UK; we've got the capacity for tremendous wealth generation for our communities; we've got the possibility of tremendous cultural development as a result of our activities; and we've got a whole plethora of initiatives which central government is taking to develop small businesses, to deal with inner city problems, and a whole host of financial incentives and inducements that we could increasingly take advantage of.

This government is very keen on talking about developing an 'enterprise culture'. Well, why don't we try and take them for once at face value and begin to think what 'developing an enterprise culture' could mean for the museum profession. I think it means a number of things. First of all surely it means being success orientated. It means looking for success and talking about success, and expecting to achieve success. It also means taking risks. It means using initiative. It means, not least, enjoying the freedom to take the decisions that need to be taken in the best interests of our museums and galleries. It also means being able to make mistakes and to learn from those mistakes.

Now, developing these kinds of attitudes doesn't mean that the museum profession shouldn't fight against the things that it doesn't like, against threats to its well-being and to the well-being of the museums that are there to serve the public. On the contrary. But it does mean that at the same time we should be getting organised to seize the opportunities that are being presented by all these changes which are taking place.

Another issue we have to face if we are talking about opportunities is that of being market-orientated, of looking actively for opportunities to exploit, of looking actively at what it is that our users actually want us to do, what services they want us to provide. Instead of – as so often happens – throwing up problems and using

those problems as road blocks, as excuses, for why we can't actually do anything.

Forbes Magazine, the American business magazine, promotes itself starkly with the slogan 'capitalist tool'. By this it means, I think, that it's a lever – it's a means of sparking off ideas which are going to make money. I think that our daily press can be used in that way – as a source of new initiatives. Let's just take three random examples from recent newspapers.

First of all the market for videos. It was noted recently that the ABC1 market for documentary videos selling at under £10 a time is increasing very rapidly. National Geographic Magazine, for example, has got a whole range of videos on sale in such places as Woolworths which are essentially documentaries about habitats or about countries throughout the world. And the important point this article was making was that although there is a tremendous demand for new videos there's actually a tremendous shortage of material to put in them. I would suggest that for any museum that's interested in communicating with a mass audience this is something that might be worth investigating – some sort of joint venture with a video distributor could be a very positive and financially lucrative thing to do.

Another recent press article focused on venture capital. John Lee, the Tourism Minister, recently announced that he was launching a venture capital fund for the leisure industry – the first venture capital fund that had ever been designed specifically for this business sector. I think it's already very telling that sites such as Jorvik and elsewhere we are seeing venture capital invested in high quality heritage projects on the basis that these are actually viable commercial enterprises.

And a third press example – prestige. We shouldn't forget that museums are perceived as tremendously prestigious places. Mohamed Al-Fayed, the Chairman and now Chief Executive of Harrods is quoted in a recent article as saying, 'It is my dream to make Harrods like a museum. We will be recreating history.' And to make Harrods like a museum he will be investing £200m over the next 5 years!

Now clearly there is not going to be a transformation of attitudes towards change overnight. But what I would want to emphasise is that there is a positive side to all the change that's taking place. This positive side is very rarely exposed and debated within the profession. If we're really going to seize the opportunities that are now being presented to us rather than being overtaken by events it needs to be far more debated than it is.

So I would suggest there are three key questions facing the profession at the moment: what business are we in; how to improve customer service; and finally, seeing change as an opportunity, rather than a threat. These issues basically involve not cash but improving managerial skills within the profession and changing attitudes within the profession. So, if we can accept these issues as some of the key ones facing the museum profession what aims could we then set ourselves for the next five years or so? I'd like to suggest that there are four that we should be looking at.

The first is to improve the quality of our museums within our *existing* resources. This raises questions for us such as, what are our real priorities? What sort of activities are really cost effective? How can we maximise our potential? And how can we get a more scientific approach to collecting?

The second aim we might set ourselves is to develop an enterprise culture and to change some of our museum values. This involves giving ourselves the freedom to take risks; focusing on delivering tangible benefits to our users and getting away from our habit of internal local authority politicing. In other words, making the measures of our success not an increased budget or an increase in the number of staff year after year but instead – quantifiable improvements in the services that we are providing to our users.

And the third aim that we could set ourselves as a profession is to diversify and popularise models of excellence.

Surely there is a need to make much more readily and freely available examples of all the excellent things which are going on in our museums. Let's make that more widely available both to professional colleagues and to committee members and Trustees so that this excellence can be emulated in other places. We have to be much better as a profession at networking information about what is good, about successful innovations. In this context we should perhaps ask ourselves whether the Area Museum Councils and the Museums & Galleries Commission have got at the moment the right kind of investment policies in place to make sure that excellence is developing and that innovation is taking place *and*, in particular, that the best of all this is satisfactorily popularised and that that experience is made as widely available as possible.

The outcome of all this might just be to change, as a result, our users' perception of the museum product. Surely, that – customer satisfaction – is the best guarantee we could possibly have of greater investment in our museums and galleries in the future.

The Rutland Dinosaur, Leicestershire Museum and Art Gallery – an exhibit involving research co-operation between Leicestershire and Argentina, Canada, France, Germany and the USA.

Leicestershire Museums and Art Galleries.

Joint Research Programmes

Patrick Boylan

Patrick Boylan is Director of Leicestershire
Museums and Art Galleries. Since 1977 he has
held various offices in the International Council of
Museums (ICOM) for which he is currently
chairman of the UK National Committee.

First can I stress that I have been given a very tight brief, which is to talk about museum-based research programmes which are primarily carried out jointly by two or more museums, and not museum-based research itself nor indeed museum research in co-operation with non-museum bodies. I must say that in looking for examples of museums co-operating with other museums in the research field, particularly in the UK, I felt at first that I was going to be able to speak for no more than five minutes rather than the allotted forty-five minutes because there are in fact very few obvious projects in this field. However, as my own research into this topic progressed things became clearer, and I now believe that there are a number of important issues to consider.

First of all, I should stress that all modern definitions of a museum include a research role as a fundamental element of the responsibilities, duties and activities of a museum, for example in the old Museums Association's Diploma definition that the museum's role was to collect, conserve, research and interpret or display collections, or in the current International Council of Museums (ICOM) definition, which stresses the research role not solely in relation to collections but to material evidence of humanity and the natural and human environment.

What then is museum research? In fact there are at least two quite different areas of activity which fall within any reasonable definition of museum research, though think it is an arguable point whether they are in fact the same thing at all.

The first is research, perhaps academic research on the collections and objects within museums, which in many cases it does not necessarily have to be museum-based at all. The second category is research relating to the museum phenomenon and both its mission and its operations: research in museology, its techniques, and indeed research into the nature and purpose of museums themselves and of the community that they serve. This of course, brings us head-on to the issue of the nature and scope of museums themselves – something which has been the subject of hot debate in many parts of the world, but perhaps not so much in Britain where an outward-looking community role has been well recognised as a vital characterisitc of successful museums for many years.

However, there are many parts of the world where such a view of museums would still not be regarded as acceptable. In some places museological research has generated a major confrontation over the social and community role of musems, particularly in France with its movement for 'new museology', and the wider development of the 'ecomuseum' phenomenon, no longer confined to France and Quebec where it originated, in which museum professionals are seeking an explicitly social role, with the 'new' museum or ecomuseum serving as an expression of social action and of integration between the environment with the community.

René Rivard, the French Canadian who has taken a leading role in this debate, claims that there is a straightforward challenge and a choice to be made between two possible models of museum. Is a museum a building containing a collection serving only the people who come to it, ie. its visitors, (which Rivard believes is the most a museum can be under current French law)? Or is a museum an institution which is based not solely on a physical building, but on the whole of a defined geographical territory, which might be at one extreme be a small village, or, in the case of the Royal Museum of Scotland, a whole country or whole nation? Is the remit of the museum solely its contents in terms of its physical objects and collections, or must its primary field of study be the whole of the natural and human heritage and environment of its defined territory? And, perhaps the biggest challenge of all, should the museum be concerned solely or mainly with serving its actual visitors, or should it be trying to serve the whole population of its geographical area, including the very significant and often large proportion of the population who are not museum visitors?

I think the issue of the basic nature of museums is very much at the forefront of not just the debate about the museum phenomenon as we approach the new century, but is already an area in which major co-operative study and research is taking place over much of the world, through groups such as the French-based 'MNES' (Muséologie Nouvelle et Experimentation Sociale), and national and international groupings of ecomuseums

and of other special interest groups with a special emphasis on the social role of museums, such as WHAM (Women's Heritage and Museums) and MAGDA (Museums and Galleries Disability Association) in the UK.

So far as practical museology research co-operation is concerned, two quite distinct areas can be identified: first, co-operation on research related to museum operations, the way in which museums run etc., and second, co-operation in collections-based research.

In relation to museums operations I suppose that far and away the most successful and important pioneering work of this kind was that done by IRGMA (the Information Retrieval Group of the Museums Association). I am delighted to see Geoffrey Lewis's contribution to these proceedings because he was a key figure in the documentation movement from the 1960s onwards, first in IRGMA and later in the Documentation Committee of ICOM. Both the UK and the international initiatives were based primarily on co-operation in documentation research and techniques between museum personnel in a very wide range of types of museums and in many different geographical locations, trying to develop an integrated approach to the key issue of documenting and recording museum collections. Subsequently, the co-operation between the Sedgwick Museum in Cambridge, and a wide range of other museums including, of course, the members of IRGMA was of crucial importance in developing practical museum computer systems, and in turn led directly to the establishment of the MDA (the Museums Documentation Association) with the invaluable help of substantial initial government funding. Over a period of more than 20 years these initiatives amounted to a substantial amount of immensely far-reaching co-operative research on how museums can and in the future should be run, and this spirit continues at both national and international levels, looking in particular at the future of museums in relation to the key late 20th century phenomenon of the information explosion which museums are part of and which at least in part the growth in museums collections represent.

Another example of this kind of national and international co-operative museological research has been central to the immense advances that have been made in recent times on museum conservation and preservation techniques. A considerable number of examples of this could be quoted, but probably much the most important has been the ICCROM international centre in Rome, even though this is not strictly speaking museum to museum co-operative research as ICCROM was established by UNESCO as an inter-governmental organisation (which thankfully the United Kingdom still does subscribe to, unlike certain other international bodies). Throughout its existence of more than 30 years ICCROM has had a central role in co-ordinating research on the preservation and conservation of humanly-produced artefacts and structures, especially works of art, antiquities, and historic buildings and structures. In addition to its research role, ICCROM has, of course, had a crucial role in co-ordinating the work of so many hundreds of scientists or conservators or museum curators the world over, and in the training of conservation, curatorial and architectural personnel.

Over the years there have been a number of other combined conservation and training centres affording facilities for fundamental research in the care of museum collections. A regional centre, perhaps less successful today but of enormous importance in the 1960s and early 1970s, was the Churibusco Conservation Institute in Mexico City which not only offered both primary training opportunities for new and prospective museum personnel and study facilities for established museum conservators, but also produced much vital information on the care of collections in Latin America and more generally in tropical regions. Now of course we have the growing influence of the Getty Conservation Institute (GCI) and the various other offshoots of the Getty Foundation (already mentioned by the Chairman in his introduction), with its huge funds. Since the establishment of the GCI only a little over three years ago, the Getty organisation has quickly become involved not just in primary conservation research in an abstract sense in its own outstanding laboratories, but in co-ordinating, funding, and generally assisting the development of research and training programmes in relation to the crucial issues in the care of collections and their long-term survival in co-operation in many dozens indeed probably hundreds, of museum personnel and individual museums around the world.

The International Council of Museums (ICOM) has itself taken a very similar role in relation to the co-ordination and sharing of research, particularly through its Conservation Committee, which has about two dozen specialist Working Groups involved in work in fields as diverse as the preservation of waterlogged wood or the conservation of mosaics. The emphasis of its work has been on the object itself and its long term preservation, conservation and restoration, which is very much international.

Perhaps, therefore, in the area of research into museum operations such as documentation and conservation we can report a considerable success story already, with further successes very much in prospect.

In preparing this paper I turned first to areas of museum-to-museum joint co-operation in collections-based research as the most obvious area, though this proved to be far from the truth, and at times I feared that my own research for this study was going to come to a rapid and permanent halt because of the lack of good examples at the practical level. However, in moments of despair I felt that I could always fall back on one quite modest personal experience, and on further reflection I think this is perhaps of wider interest in relation to the theme I have been asked to review, because it involved co-operation between people in three very different museums (on two different continents), and which indicates that even very small local museums can make a useful contribution in much larger projects.

The story in fact began in the 1820s, when scientists in this country started to find fragmented and smashed-up bones with strange markings on them in cave deposits, first in the north of England in Kirkdale Cave northeast of York, and then in other parts of Britain, followed soon by similar discoveries on the continent as well. By some outstanding inductive reasoning the scientist working on the original and many of the subsequent discoveries, William Buckland, the first Professor of Geology at Oxford, decided that the highly distinctive damage must be the results of predation by carnivores and (in the words used light-heartedly at the time) quickly 'convicted' the fossil Cave Hyaena as the culprit.

This interpretation did not fit in at all with the current view of the cowardly laughing hyaena of the popular literature of the day, and Buckland had no direct observations to support his reasoning, but his argument seemed quite overwhelming to many of the leading national and international scientists of the time. Indeed when, in 1826, a British Officer in the Indian Army exploring the hills behind Poona (where else?) found the den of some Indian hyaenas, they proved to be behaving 'exactly as though they had attended two courses of Professor Buckland's Oxford lectures', as one disgruntled critic put it at the time. Buckland's explanation of the classic and very distinctive damage to a wide range of different Pleistocene bones was largely unchallenged, though never fully investigated again until the 1950s. Then similar phenomena were discovered during excavations of some very important early Hominid sites in southern Africa, particularly at Swartkrans which was producing bones and teeth of Australopithecines. At this point a whole group of South African-based anthropologists argued that the hyaena hypothesis was complete nonsense, claiming that hyaenas do not do this sort of thing, and that the very distinctive bone damage both in the South African sites and in the original classic sites of Western Europe must be the result deliberate bone toolmaking and/or butchery by early man. It was further suggested that the early scientists, particularly Buckland, who developed the original hyaena theory were in fact religious bigots and frauds who could not face up to the true nature of early Man before The Fall – who had been in reality a barbaric savage who savagely smashed bones in this distinctive way, and not the idyllic creature described in the beginning of the Book of Genesis. In their eyes the whole of this hyaena theory was not just entirely false, it was positively fraudulent as the result of unscientific and unprincipled religious prejudice.

It was against this background that I was persuaded by Dr Antony Sutcliffe of the British Museum (Natural History) to begin work as part of a small group of people from three museums on two continents: the British Museum (Natural History) with Tony Sutcliffe, the Coryndon Museum in Nairobi (now the National Museum of Kenya) with a research student, Christopher Buckland-Wright (no relation!) under Louis and Mary Leakey, and me working first in the Hull Museums in Yorkshire and latterly at Exeter.

Our small and entirely informal international team, operated at a very simple and low-tech level, without expensive equipment and with fairly minimal travel budgets. The Natural History Museum helped to fund Tony Sutcliffe's fieldwork in eastern and southern Africa looking at what actually happens in and around spotted hyaena dens and lairs. The Coryndon Museum financed anatomical research by Chris Buckland-Wright on the beast itself, both live and dissected: its structure and especially the enormous neck and skull muscles which enable it to smash the bones of animals far larger than itself, and what actually happened to bones and bone splinters in the beast's stomach. My own role was to work on both an historical review of the original evidence and sources of the 1820s and to undertake a detailed re-examination and re-evaluation of the surviving historic collections from Buckland's original excavations now scattered through fifteen institutions (including a few items in the Royal Museum of Scotland). Our small and entirely informal group was eventually able to put together an overwhelming series of conclusions in each of these different areas to demonstrate that contrary to then current confident assertions by the South African anthropologists, the living hyaena does live and behave in just the way predicted, largely from the Yorkshire fossil evidence, almost a century and a half earlier, that its anatomy is that of a highly specialised machine more than capable of smashing and consuming bones in the way predicted, and that far from being blind (or fraudulent) religious fanatics, Buckland and those of his generation what accepted his hyaena den theory were outstanding and unbiased scientists anxious to discover the truth.

We also established, I think very firmly, not only that the then fashionable South African interpretation of classic hyaena bone damage as evidence of primitive tool-making by early hominids was fundamentally wrong, but also that Buckland's original research in the early 1820s marked the foundation of both modern palaeoecology and taxonomy studies, and also of Pleistocene vertebrate palaeontology.

This is a very brief and much simplified case study of one co-operative research project between different museums of which I had personal experience, but in fact there are many other examples of national and international museums co-operating in similar ways, including a welcome trend these days towards co-operation with museums in developing countries, as well as many very long-standing relationships with those of developed countries. For example, in the British Museum (Natural History) entomologists have been working closely with the major natural history museums of Australia for at least fifty years, and in more recent times, the Mexican National Ecology Institute with the Mexico City Natural History Museum has established a crucial partnership, again in entomology, with a number of United States institutions, including the Smithsonian Institution, which assist not just with joint research as such, but also with some modest practical assistance to institutions in a country in a desperate state because of the collapse of the national currency.

Also in Central America there are close research links in the study and curation of pre-Columbian art and archaeology, including pottery, and particularly the study of the magnificent Central American jade cultures, between the Jade Museum of Costa Rica and the University Museum in Denver, Colorado.

Looking at even longer distances the Natural History Museum in La Plata in Argentina which has a superb vertebrate fossil collections has now developed links with the National Science Museum in Tokyo, both in research projects and also the loan of exhibits. Here, it is interesting to see assistance in very practical terms in the form of much new specialist equipment for the geological laboratories in La Plata and (extremely useful when you are collecting large dinosaur fossils a thousand kilometres south of your museum in a remote part of Patagonia), two Toyota Land Cruisers! Indeed our geologists in Leicestershire are working quite closely with curators and researchers at the Museum at La Plata on particular aspects of Jurassic dinosaurs common to both Patagonia and Leicestershire. Also, in Leicestershire we have close links with the University Museum at Tubigen, West Germany, on Jurassic marine reptiles, such as ichthyosaurs, plesiosaurs and marine crocodiles, and their preservation. So there are possibilities for co-operation on international basis even for more modest local museums, not just the major national and international institutions.

This kind of simple but valuable co-operation is by no means restricted to the sciences of course. In fine art, to take another example, the Yale Centre for British Art, funded largely by Paul Mellon, has had a very close working relationship for the best part of twenty years with most of the leading UK national and provincial art galleries in the documentation, investigation, and identification of British Art from the 16th century onwards. Another fine art example is the Rembrandt project, a long-term co-operative research project aimed at the definitive identification and cataloguing of all actual and claimed Rembrandt paintings, which is led by the Rijksmuseum in Amsterdam, but in partnership with professional colleagues in universities and museums in many other parts of the world.

Also, within the fine art and applied art fields especially, every year we have large numbers of examples of collaborative research projects, many of them of a high academic and professional order, in preparation for important temporary exhibitions mounted jointly by two or more museums or galleries. Obviously, all of these many kinds of collaboration are very much to be welcomed. This is particularly so in relation to major expensive temporary exhibitions: if museums can still afford 'blockbusters' at all, few can afford to put them on in just one location, and even fewer can afford to simply throw away the massive amount of preparatory research rather than produce a permanent, well-researched, scholarly record.

Perhaps of even more far reaching importance, is the example of collections research studies. For example, over the past twelve or thirteen years since the establishment first of the Geological Curators Group, followed by the several other specialists groups within the UK museum orbit, we have seen the development of extremely important collections research projects. The Geological Curators Group itself has produced an excellent series of deeply-researched reports and very provocative studies about both the state of geological collections and their history and the identity of the people who created the large number of UK geological collections, both large and small. Very recently the Biological Curators Group's collections research study has been published by the Museums Association as *Biological Collections UK*, and many other Specialist Groups are also carrying out the same kind of work, including currently the Museum Ethnographers' Group, again mentioned this morning, and the Society of Museum Archaeologists.

May I at this point ask a question? Are we in fact in these examples talking about *museum* collaborative research, or are we talking about the *museum staff* collaborative research projects? Far more fundamentally, within many of those museums where a tremendous amount of very valuable research work of this and other kinds is being done, are these activities accepted as an essential part of the job, or just as at best a harmless eccentricity – something staff can be allowed to do when they have nothing better to fill their nine to five day, or – even more cynically – proof that the museum is both over-staffed and under-worked? There are many different answers to that question. In the case of many of the national and university museums the requirements of the post in many of the scientific fields in particular, especially at the early stages of career are predominantly research-based. Research ability, potential and contribution can be a key factor in any appraisal, promotion or indeed the original recruitment, in such posts.

However, I think there is undoubtedly a major divide between the national and university museums on the one side and 'the rest'. Recent confidential discussion and information exchange within the United Kingdom Group of Directors of Museums, shows that research responsibilities and obligations are extremely rare in local authority and independent museums. Probably only four or five large or medium-sized museums had any such obligation written into staff contracts. One exception is my own institution where (with the full support of the local politicians responsible for the Service, I should stress), the Director, Deputy, the four Assistant Directors and all Keepers, have had research responsibilities explicitly written into their contracts and requirements of the job since the establishment of the Leicestershire Museums, Art Galleries and Records Service since its establishment in 1973.

A further, and perhaps even more important issue is the question of whether museums, large or small, are prepared to provide proper support for museum research, regardless of whatever lip-service may be paid to research in any statement of objectives, corporate plan or job description. Such essential support is possibly even more scarce than any written requirement to actually undertake research. The fact is, again, that few other than national or university museums allow any time off for research at all.

I often joke that in the case of my own terms of employment by Leicestershire I am allowed one and a half days per week for research: every Saturday afternoon and all day Sunday (providing, of course, that there are no special weekend events that I should appear at or backlog to clear on my desk!), but even with a very busy job and heavy workload it is still possible to undertake worthwhile research if you have reasonable back-up support such as secretarial help together with some practical and financial assistance. However hardly any museums outside the national and university sectors have significant funds for either travel or research expenses such as equipment, or even for re-training and career development, such as assisting staff with the now very considerable cost of undertaking a higher degree, and to the best of knowledge virtually no museum, public or independent, have any sort of scheme for staff sabbaticals, although I think that perhaps one or two of the university museums where the professional staff have university teaching staff conditions, may be an exception.

This is in marked contrast with an area such as primary and secondary school teaching in England and Wales, where central government provides very substantial sums for in-service training and re-training of teachers in the widest sense, of which a significant amount is devoted to the funding of sabbaticals and research leave. I am particularly aware of this in the case of my own Leicestershire local education authority because we have teachers on their one year sabbaticals or research grants who actually want to come and work in the museum for that period.

Within the museum field, in contrast, with the exception of a tiny number of museums, mainly the major national institutions and a small number of university museums, any commitment or obligation to research is in a definition is honoured more in the breach, rather than the action.

Where do we.go in the future? The Museums and Galleries Commission's Hale Report on *Museum Training and Career Structure* has been referred to earlier and I do not really apologise to Chris Newbery of the Commission for saying that I think the section in relation to career structure and status of staff is perhaps the least satisfactory of an otherwise excellent report. Perhaps the most important recommendation in this section is that further research on this thorny issue is necessary and I was delighted that Graeme Farnell has now managed to put together for the Museums Association a funding package for further research on career structure.

Despite my earlier, more general, comments, I feel that the Hale Report certainly has some excellent, practical ideas in relation to the major challenge that we are facing in terms of the (dare I say it?) fossilisation of promotion prospects. So many outstanding young people were appointed and promoted rapidly in the massive UK museum expansion of the late 1960s through to the mid 1970s that we now have a situation in which promotion prospects are pretty well nil, in large numbers of institutions. In my own Department we have eighteen Keepers or equivalent across the various branches of the Service, which covers not just museums, but also includes the county Record Office, a Museum Education Service and a very large scale environmental research operation, a total of perhaps 6% – 7% of the total professional museum jobs outside London. However, the next Keepership on the curatorial side which will definitely become vacant through the natural process of retirement will not be available for another eighteen years. Try telling that to an absolutely brilliant person in their early thirties who only ten years ago would have probably been in a Directorship or certainly in a senior curatorship at this stage. I therefore very much welcome the Hale Report's response of recommending that means be found to establish opportunities such as sabbaticals, and I regard as especially important the imaginative suggestion of a panel of experienced museum professionals, perhaps recently retired people, available to look after small museums while staff are undertaking training or otherwise absent in relation to career development opportunities. This would be very beneficial indeed.

This view is of course very much echoing Prof. Martin Kemp's plea for sabbaticals and secondments, both between museum and museum, particularly but not exclusively between smaller museums and larger ones, and between museums and academic institutions, but I think there could well be a lot of scope for and value in secondments in the other direction. Maybe some of the larger museum and academic institutions, despite their desperate financial and other problems, might be in a slightly better position to actually lend someone to go and spend three weeks assisting with a simple research project and staff training exercise in a small local museum, rather than try to find a relief curator to go to the small town while its one museum professional goes away to London or Edinburgh.

I do think though that in this respect the larger institutions: the national and major university museums together with the leading local authority museums, have an important responsibility to the profession as a whole. This of course, is stressed in the ICOM *Code of Professional Ethics*, adopted last year, in which the commitment to the development of the profession as a whole, and assisting newer entrants to the profession, is seen as very much an ethical consideration. There are of course, some very satisfactory examples being set in this field: the National Gallery in London has for quite a number of years from time to time offered conservation sabbaticals in particular.

Where do we go from here? I think the Royal Museum of Scotland and its predecessor constituent institutions have a long and honourable role in Scotland in relation to the smaller institutions, as indeed have the Glasgow Museums and Art Galleries and the National Gallery of Scotland. I am delighted that the Museums and Galleries Commission's Report on Museums in Scotland has once again emphasised the potential of the national institutions in assisting the rest of the profession, but I think it has to be accepted that Scotland, Wales and indeed Northern Ireland – all of which have interdisciplinary national museums – are frankly in a much more favourable position than England, which has up to now had no overall national museum, (the new regional National Museums and Galleries on Merseyside being an interesting development), but has instead about two dozen or so highly specialised individual and in some cases individualistic institutions.

I accept that all of the national institutions are under great financial pressure which regrettably, may lead to more rather than less restrictive and introspective positions in relation to co-operation with other museums. The sort of high charges for the identification of specimens and for working space for visiting researchers currently under consideration at the British Museum (Natural History) are a measure of the desperation of the institution faced with its current financial problems. They result from a climate of opinion in which short-term commercial benefits seem to be the main criteria in determining the nation's funding of fundamental research, from the natural environment to space science, and in which unquantifiable longer-term potential is a very low priority.

Finally, in my view, research whether in museums or out of them depends ultimately not on rules, regulations, staff conditions or even budgets, but on the existence of a clear commitment to research. One of the smallest city museum services in eastern England, that of Peterborough, may not be very well-known even in UK museum circles, but over the past five or six years has developed a world-wide fame within two different fields of geology, because of the research work and commitment of two successive Deputy Curators within an institution with only four or five staff.

Success or failure in these areas depends eventually to an enormous extent on commitment and a willingness to co-operate. The theme of this publication is co-operation, and we need to look for that co-operation in all areas of our activity and see it as a professional responsibility to offer co-operation and assistance. What is needed is not just a one-way system under which the large institutions assist the small, but a much broader one for the mutual benefit of our national and local museums and related institutions as a whole. Further, coming back to the current French debate about the fundamental nature of museums referred to previously, the ultimate beneficiary of our efforts should be the public that we serve today and, equally important, the people not yet born. In our curatorial, conservation and research work we are in fact serving not just the present, we should be conscious at all time of the fact that we are also serving countless generations in future centuries. We need to accept that it is a basic responsibility under the ethical principles of our profession to seek and develop professional co-operation in all areas and I commend this principle to you.

Lessons from France for Museums in the United Kingdom. Central Hall of the Musée d'Orsay, Paris, shortly after its opening in 1986.   *Maria Newbery.*

National and Local Museums in the United Kingdom

Geoffrey Lewis

Geoffrey Lewis is Director of Museum Studies in the University of Leicester. Previous appointments include directorships of the Merseyside County and Sheffield City Museums. He has recently been elected to a second term as President of the International Council of Museums (ICOM) and is a past President of the Museums Association.

Introduction

Inter-museum cooperation is one of a number of different forms of professional self-help to be found among museums in Britain. Indeed, compared with many other professions, the doctrine of self-help has been almost an obsession as reference to museum history soon reveals; consider also the number of organizations concerned with museums in relation to the size of the profession. Perhaps this obsession is related to the professional fanaticism mentioned by Crispin Paine (p.   ). For an emerging profession such an obsession may be understandable. The Museums Association however celebrates its centenary in eighteen months time. Public museums have been in existence for three hundred years, and even if you dismiss the Ashmolean and the British Museum as aberrations there still remains a solid core of public museum service for a century and a half. The idea of self-help, however, remains a significant feature of the museum scene.

This paper considers, therefore, the broader concept of self-help among museums, some of the principles involved and their implications. It then examines a few examples of inter-museum cooperation. For contrast some comment will be made on the support facilities of the museums financed through the Ministry of Culture in France, not to make any complex comparisons but rather to provide a foil to an otherwise somewhat insular view; for this information I am indebted to Bruno Suzzarelli[1]. In doing this, some aspects of the United Kingdom system, if system is the right word to use, may be given a different dimension.

The idea of self-help

Self-help presents a cosy concept of caring collaboration in the museum world. It sounds well and is generally acceptable politically, even if a little money has to be found to set it up and, perhaps rather more rarely, to maintain it. Two major schemes, the Area Museum Councils and the Consultative Committees, both of which commenced on the basis of self-help and continue to some extent on this basis have already been discussed; others have been referred to also in this publication. What follows by way of introduction is not intended in any way to detract from those successful schemes already described or for that matter inter-museum cooperation generally. It is necessary, however, to ask the sort of questions that any manager would ask automatically of the work in hand. Are objectives being met? Has the idea of self-help been entirely beneficial? Is the profession richer for it or has it been counter-productive? Indeed is this the way forward to higher standards of performance and better public service or do such schemes tend to obscure the non-viability of certain of the receiving museums?

There are two broad types of professional self-help. The first operates on the basis that the combined resources of two or more museums can produce a better job to their common advantage than any of them singly. This is a widely accepted practice and has much to commend it. The objective is clear and there is a singleness of purpose about it. However, where a museum is deficient in the resources necessary to achieve a generally accepted museum function, and another museum or agency provides assistance, then a different situation arises. Two objectives will have to be met, those of the supplying and receiving museums. What those objectives are will vary: the supplier may be altruistic with self-help as the goal; other goals may be scholarly, economic or perhaps less obvious. Whatever the goal, it presupposes that the supplier has the knowledge and skills to offer to an acceptable professional standard and the spare capacity to provide them. For the receiver the gain will almost certainly be in terms of an improved service. Whether this is a temporary or permanent gain depends on the nature of the deficiency but regrettably the help normally provides only a transitory respite which the receiver is unable to maintain for lack of resouces – the very reason that led to the seeking of self-help in the first

place. Sometimes, of course, such assistance can highlight potential to an extent that the appropriate authorities are persuaded to provide support on a permanent basis.

There is a third form of self-help. This, however, does not involve another party. My own training for the Museums Association Diploma in the 'Fifties assumed that curators should design as well as display, conserve and restore as well as do many other things deemed appropriate for a curator to do. Now, thirty years on, those days are generally considered to be long since past. And yet they linger. There is still a very broad streak of the amateur, the dilettante, in the profession. It reflects itself in the quite common delight expressed at the 'practical' nature of museum work. Yes, many of us still enjoy doing 'a bit of art-work', designing a display, restoring a pot – or an engine. It is all great fun. But the jack-of-all-trades approach can be an insidious form of self-help and normally results from scarce resources with no possibility of support from another museum or agency. There is nothing in this do-it-yourself approach which will raise public confidence in the profession to which it entrusts its cultural heritage or, for that matter, improve and develop that professionalism.

All this raises some fundamental issues. What are our objectives? They must surely embrace the preservation of the heritage and its interpretation. Our clientele for the preservation of the heritage is the world at large: our collections are the heritage of humankind. When it comes to interpreting the heritage, however, our target audiences may well be varied: scholarly or lay; minority interests or child; group or individual and so on. If we cannot operate in these two key areas – preservation and interpretation – in a professional manner then have we any right to be involved at all? Now it is, of course, in these two areas that the Scottish Museums Council and its sister organizations in England and Wales have contributed so much, through their services, to such vastly improved standards over the last quarter of a century. This is highly commendable. The main beneficiaries have been the smaller museums. I spent the first eleven years of my career in a small museum as the only full-time professional member of staff and can testify to the real boost that even a small grant or service can make to that museum and its staff. There must, however, be grave misgivings if there is no curator on the spot to maintain those collections and displays or, indeed, to provide personal contact with the museum's clientele. I am sorry to see that the recently approved guidelines for the national registration scheme for museums does not insist on this. The concept of the peripatetic curator, pioneered and tried for a time here in Scotland, only goes so far in meeting this requirement.

It is necessary to recognise the issue of self-help for what it is. Aspects of it can form a particularly vicious circle. It can produce a short-term illusion of improved standards when in fact it is a veneer covering a deteriorating performance and lack of professionalism. As self-help increases between museums, more inroads are made into the time and effort available in the giving museums. There may be very sound reasons for involvement in self-help (as we have used the term here), be they political, economic or social but let us at least be aware of what we are doing. Unless there is a common objective among the participants and continuing professional support to maintain and develop the work, it is unlikely to be contributing to improved standards or to professional development in the long term.

Inter-Museum Cooperation

I have purposely interpreted the theme given to me as inter-museum cooperation. Otherwise there could be an unwarranted assumption that working with museums is one way: from national to local. Further I have no wish to imply that cooperation should be restricted to certain types of museum. If our common objectives are to preserve and interpret the nation's heritage, this is of sufficient significance and magnitude to require cooperation between all those involved. On the other hand, if the evidence provided in the Williams[2], Bute[3] and Miles[4] Reports is any guide, the cooperation between museums is largely of an informal character unless channelled through the Scottish Museums Council. In such circumstances, the best approach would seem to be to examine the main museum functions for areas of potential collaboration.

Collection management

Collection management on the one hand is the most difficult area of inter-museum cooperation in certain respects and yet in others the most prolific. The difficulties arise over the issue of collecting itself. We might say that because of the human propensity to acquire – a vital aspect in the formation of museums and an essential trait of the curator – that this is inevitable. There are, however, other factors at play, not least the natural reaction to perceive an acquisition in terms of its usage. If there was a far greater clarity among curatorial staff of the museum's primary role – the preservation of the nation's heritage – and that collectively we are working to this common goal, then I believe there would be greater understanding.

Strangely, in Scotland, a very important ingredient exists to help this which is denied to curators elsewhere in the United Kingdom. As far as archaeological material is concerned the principles relating to *bona vacantia* apply which gives such material a public status from which a custodial responsibility follows. However with this, and especially on the issue of treasure trove, there could be much greater cooperation, a factor particularly emphasised in the Miles Report[4]. Apart from this there is in the museums of Scotland a considerable body of curatorial expertise, mainly but not exclusively in the larger museums, which is clearly available on an informal basis. Whether this should be formalized is a matter for discussion, particularly as Miles suggests that as far the national museums are concerned, there is a feeling that they are 'an unapproachable class apart'. As far as the Local Museums Purchase Fund administered by the Royal Museum of Scotland is concerned I regard this more as an agency than inter-museum cooperation.

In France the museum scene is very different and dominated by the Paris-based Direction des Musées de France (DMF). The DMF has very strong legal powers that require it to supervise and control the national museums of France and also some thirty-three key municipal museums which are known as musées classées. All of these museums are run by cuators who have received a common training at the École du Louvre. There is therefore, at least in theory, a common perception of the museum and its role in French society among all the key practitioners. This actually goes further in that the curatorial staff of over a thousand other provincial museums – some of them independent – are also subject to vetting by DMF before they can be appointed. These are the musées controlées. So, to all intent and purpose, the majority of French curators receive a common training. It is worth noting here the Williams Report[2] comments on training for national museum staff, recommending that curatorial staff should be encouraged to study for the Museums Association Diploma.

As far as acquisitions in French museums are concerned the matter rests entirely with the DMF. The control is considerable. It is responsible for issuing export permits. It can pre-empt sales at public auction in the name of the State by matching the highest bid. It holds the total purchase budget for the Ministry of Culture museums (about £6.3m in 1986), there being no allocations to individual museums. The decision-making process is interesting. It is a collegiate approach whereby a Commission involving representatives of each museum – known among our French colleagues as the 'Republic of Curators' – considers each museum's bid on its merits. French curators would argue that this approach gives museum staff a sense of belonging to the organization and that the decisions made are competent ones, based on the best expertise available.

The same approach – decision by a commission of curators – is also taken on a number of other professional matters, among them the conservation of works of art and the making of long-term loans. On the question of long-term loans for exhibitions outside the holding museum, decisions in the United Kingdom may be by the governing body or delegated to the Director. Inter-museum cooperation on travelling exhibitions received a severe blow ten years ago when the Victoria and Albert Museum closed its Regional Services Department and this vacuum has not been filled, despite noble efforts by a number of Area Museum Services. Because of the quality of the material held by the national museums in Scotland, the Miles Report[4] recommended the creation of a new travelling exhibitions unit linked to the national museums, a recommendation particularly supported by the Scottish Museums Council. But the problem with self-help is the need for two willing partners and neither my reading of the Miles Report nor the reference in the Bute Report to the possibility of long loans 'on occasion' inspires confidence in the progressing of the scheme. There will have to be a real commitment by those involved.

On other elements in collection management, inter-museum cooperation exists in the documentation of museum collections, the provision of research support and in the availability of specialist conservation services. Some of the latter are provided by museums acting as agents to the Area Museum Services where dual objectives could be the source of conflict unless properly managed. The idea of a national inventory of Scottish museum collections has been mooted in more than one of the recent official reports. Even if initially only concerned with key pieces of Scotland's heritage it would make available a body of information to subject specialists and the public, to say nothing of curators themselves, in a form which people increasingly are expecting their data to be. Museums are massive holders of information – much of it the primary evidence for a number of disciplines – and we should be responding actively to the new technology available before we are overtaken by events. It has relevance not just as a public service but in providing internal management information systems which museums, with their heavily labour-intensive operations, would do well to heed.

Museum services

There are many areas of potential inter-museum cooperation in the public services. These range from the provision of items on loan for exhibition or display purposes, to joint or multiple cooperation in the preparation and circulation of travelling exhibitions, as already referred to. Similarly in the fields of education, information services and the increasing number of ancillary services being provided by museums there are areas ripe for mutually beneficial collaboration. At a time when such acronyms as VFM – value for money – figure in our lives to say nothing of the need for alternative sources of revenue to be found, the opportunities for joint publishing, combined marketing and trading need close examination.

At this point it would be useful to return to France and introduce ourselves to another body associated with the Direction des Musées de France: the Réunion des Musées Nationaux (RMN). This is the public services and commercial arm of DMF, the Director of the Museums of France being responsible for both organizations. RMN had a turnover of about £14m on a £30m budget in 1985. No, it is not a new company created to generate revenue to help ameliorate the contemporary financial climate. It dates to 1895 and was set up to receive the revenue from admission

charges which in turn were used to acquire new works of art for the national museum. It was, and is, a mechanism to overcome the legal requirement that income generated by a State department should go direct to the exchequer, an issue familiar to a British audience. Today the RMN is responsible for the major temporary exhibitions, for commercial operations involving publications and the reproduction of specimens for sale and generally administering the museums' business operations. From its surplus, four of the French national museums shared about £4m last year. It has also contributed a similar sum to the Grand Louvre project.

Concluding thoughts

Where well-founded, imaginative cooperation between museums has been established, it tends to flourish to the benefit of both of the institutions involved as well as the public. This, however, relates to situations where two or more institutions recognise that by their combined efforts they can achieve far more than they could singly. Where museum provision is failing to meet minimum standards, however, it is unlikely that any lasting benefit can result from inter-museum cooperation. This raises fundamental questions about the practice of self-help in this situation. It is to be hoped that the minimum standards set through the Museums and Galleries Commission's new Registration Scheme will contribute by identifying and hopefully rectifying some of the problems, but it is doubtful whether the scheme goes far enough. Some museums will fall short of the requirements, however, particularly among the two hundred or so new museums of the last ten years, which incidentally represent about half of Scotland's museums.

In addition museums are not immune to social, economic and political forces. A period of financial austerity or a sudden down-turn in Scotland's tourist industry could have a major impact on them. Another factor to watch is when the first flush of enthusiasm among some of the new independent museums begins to wane. These are pessimistic comments to make towards the end of a conference. But history has a habit of repeating itself. Do you recall what happened to the nineteenth-century Society museums? Planning for such eventualities and consideration of the nature of any self-help that might be offered should form part of any emergency planning undertaken. This will also make demands on inter-museum collaboration. The minimum requirement, however, will be to ensure that important elements of the national heritage held by museums threatened with closure are secured for the future.

References

[1] Suzzarelli, Bruno *Management in French museums*, unpublished paper presented to British Council seminar, Leicester, 1987.

[2] Williams, Alwyn *A heritage for Scotland: Scotland's national museums and galleries, the next 25 years*, HMSO, Edinburgh, 1981.

[3] Bute, The Earl of *Report by the Museums Advisory Board*, Scottish Education Department, Edinburgh, 1985.

[4] Miles, Hamish *Museums in Scotland*, Museums and Galleries Commission, HMSO, London, 1986.

Other Publications

New Museums

A start-up guide

By Timothy Ambrose

'A wealth of sensible advice valid throughout the whole of the UK – and indeed beyond. Crisply written and illustrated by amusingly apposite cartoons' Heritage Outlook.

In recent years there has been a surge of interest in developing new museums throughout the UK — in Scotland, for example, some 200 museums have been established in the last ten years. Museums are fun — but they bring with them financial, legal and moral responsibilities.
This guide gives a realistic view of the challenges faced in starting up and running a successful independent museum, and answers some of the questions often asked by those involved. It covers everything from staff training to insurance, and from heat, light and humidity to teas and toilet facilities.

Scottish Museums Council
February 1987 198×210 mm 64 pages illus
ISBN 0 11 493120 8 Paperback **£5.50**

The American Museum Experience

In search of excellence

What can the American experience teach us about new approaches to museum fund-raising, staff training, education programmes? This book presents a unique view of some imaginative work going on in America, through the eyes of six directors of leading American museum organisations. Bringing together the papers presented to a major 1985 conference, it explores innovative responses to problems confronting museums of all types as they plan for the 21st century. With museums now increasingly recognised not only as educational and leisure facilities, but also as contributors to the wealth and health of our society, the book has a relevance beyond the museum profession itself. Planners, politicians, leisure providers and educationalists too will find it a source of stimulation and enjoyment.

Scottish Museums Council
1986 198×210 mm 100 pages illus
ISBN 0 11 492487 2 Paperback **£8.95**